New Politics,

New Parliament?

A review of parliamentary
modernisation since 1997

University of Plymouth Library

2005

New Politics, New Parliament?

A review of parliamentary modernisation since 1997

Text and graphics © Hansard Society 2005

Published by the Hansard Society, LSE, 9 Kingsway, London, WC2B 6XF
Tel: 0207 395 4000, Fax: 0207 395 4008, hansard@hansard.lse.ac.uk

The Hansard Society is an independent, non-partisan educational charity, which exists to promote effective parliamentary democracy.

The Hansard Society's Parliament and Government Programme works on all issues relating to the reform of Parliament, engagement between Parliament and the public and promoting effective parliamentary government through a range of conferences, publications, public and private meetings.

We set the agenda on parliamentary reform through our work with parliamentarians and others to improve the operation of parliamentary government and encourage greater accessibility and closer engagement with the public.

For information about other Hansard Society publications visit our website at www.hansardsociety.org.uk

The views expressed in this publication are those of the authors. The Hansard Society, as an independent non-party organisation, is neither for nor against. The Society is, however, happy to publish these views and to invite analysis and discussion of them.

ISBN 0 900432 62 4

Cover design and photography by Ross Ferguson
Printed and bound in Great Britain by Banjo Design & Print Limited

Authors

Alex Brazier is Senior Research Fellow on the Parliament and Government Programme, Hansard Society.

Matthew Flinders is Senior Lecturer in Politics and Sub-Dean, Faculty of Social Sciences, University of Sheffield.

Declan McHugh is Director of the Parliament and Government Programme, Hansard Society.

Table of Contents

List of Appendices

Appendix 1 : List of Interviews

Appendix 2 : Modernisation Committee Reports 1997-2005

Appendix 3 : Leaders of the House 1997-2005

Appendix 4 : Core Tasks of Select Committees, adopted by the Commons in May 2002

Appendix 5 : Government Refusal to Release Documents to Select Committees 2001-2005

Appendix 6 : Analysis of Applications for Information Under the Code of Practice on Access to Official Information 1998-2002

Appendix 7 : Written Parliamentary Questions (WPQs) and Ministerial Blocking

Appendix 8 : Government Defeats in the House of Lords 1992-2004

Appendix 9 : Key Reports and Government Replies

Appendix 10 : Major Changes to House Sitting Arrangements since 1998

Appendix 11 : Use of Sub-Committees and Turnover of Membership in Six Selected Cases

Appendix 12 : Parliamentary Scrutiny Reforms 2001-2005

Preface

The Hansard Society has a long interest in the operation of parliamentary democracy and has produced, over more than sixty years, a number of publications examining parliamentary government in the UK and around the world. The Society has also, through its Commissions, examined various aspects of the UK political process with a view to recommending reforms. Three of the most recent Commissions focused specifically on the Westminster Parliament. In 1992, the Rippon Commission examined the legislative process in its entirety – its report, *Making the Law*, becoming one of the most authoritative and influential texts on the law making process (updated in Brazier A. (ed), *Parliament, Politics and Law Making* 2004). In 2001, the Hansard Society Commission on Parliamentary Scrutiny, chaired by Lord Newton of Braintree, looked at Parliament's non-legislative functions and suggested ways to make government more accountable. It, too, was an influential report and is credited with having had an important bearing on recent parliamentary reforms. Most recently, in 2005, the report of the Puttnam Commission – *Members Only? Parliament in the Public Eye* – has suggested ways that Parliament might increase its ability to communicate its work to the world outside. While smaller in scale than these three Commissions, *New Politics, New Parliament?* covers similar ground by identifying and assessing changes to parliamentary procedure and practice since 1997 with a view to suggesting pragmatic options for reform. It is now eight years since Labour entered office with a commitment to 'modernise' the Westminster Parliament. As a new Parliament begins its work, following the election of a third successive Labour Government, the Hansard Society believes that this is an appropriate moment to take stock of the nature, extent and overall impact of the 'modernisation' process in order to plot the next steps that should be taken.

Acknowledgements

The authors of this report would like to thank a number of people who kindly agreed to be interviewed as part of this inquiry: Anne Campbell MP, Rt Hon Robin Cook MP, Rt Hon Gwyneth Dunwoody MP, Mark Fisher MP, Rt Hon Eric Forth MP, Rt Hon Peter Hain MP, Prof. Robert Hazell, Oliver Heald MP, Baroness Jay, Lord Norton of Louth, Peter Riddell, Joan Ruddock MP, Dr Meg Russell, Lord Sheldon, Sir Nicholas Winterton MP, Tony Wright MP, Sir George Young MP. Appendix 1 provides details of when these interviews were conducted; where quotations in the text of the report are not specifically referenced, this denotes that they derive from the interviews.

We would also like to thank a number of civil servants and Commons clerks for their insights, as well as Oonagh Gay and Richard Kelly in the House of Commons Library, who provided us with valuable information, research and advice. In addition, we are thankful to colleagues at the Hansard Society and University of Sheffield for their help and involvement, and give particular mention to Ragnhild Handagard and Vidya Ram who helped produce the final manuscript.

Finally, the authors are very grateful to the Nuffield Foundation for funding this project.

Executive Summary

- Parliament matters. The view of Parliament as being irrelevant, powerless or tangential to modern politics and government is a wholly misleading caricature. However, rapid change within government, society and to Britain's broader constitutional architecture has to some degree left Parliament behind.

- In 1997 Labour came to power committed to modernising Parliament in order to make the institution more effective, shift the balance of power between Parliament and the executive, and improve the public perception of Parliament. Although a number of significant reforms have been implemented, particularly during the 2001-2005 Parliament, there has not been a fundamental shift in the balance of power between Parliament and the executive.

- In general, modernisation-as-efficiency has had more success than modernisation-as-scrutiny. That bias largely resulted from the failure of the Select Committee on the Modernisation of the House of Commons to set out a coherent end-point for modernisation.

- With no clear objectives defined, the role of the Leader of the House as Chair of the Modernisation Committee became the dominant factor that influenced the course of the Committee's work.

- Between 1997 and 2001, although there were a number of important changes to the legislative process, the Modernisation Committee was steered away from addressing issues concerning the accountability of the executive. However, a confluence of factors occurred in the summer of 2001 that opened a 'window of opportunity' in relation to parliamentary reform, which the then Leader of the House was able to exploit.

- Key developments included the introduction of additional payments to select committee chairs, reforms to select committees and parliamentary questions and the bi-annual appearance of the Prime Minister before the Liaison Committee. The impact of these reforms is not yet fully known or apparent although the long-term effect of the reforms may be to strengthen Parliament in ways that the Government did not intend or anticipate when they were passed.

- This audit of parliamentary modernisation reveals a number of 'cracks and wedges' in terms of important first-step reforms that may now be built upon and extended during future Parliaments. It is in this vein that this report sets out a pragmatic and realistic reform agenda that builds upon recent reforms and proposals that are currently under review.

- The modernisation process has delivered some tangible results, including significant changes to Parliament's legislative process and its scrutiny functions as well as improvements to the way that Westminster is organised. However, further reform is required and this report makes a number of recommendations for change.

- Parliament's authority rests on public confidence. If it is to restore this confidence it must take advantage of the current momentum for reform and build on recent reforms, not just to shift the balance of power between Parliament and the executive, but to close the growing gulf between Parliament and the public.

1 | Introduction

It is now eight years since Labour won a landslide election victory to end 18 consecutive years of Conservative Government. One aspect of the incoming Labour Government's programme was a commitment to radical reform of the political process, including proposals to 'modernise' the operation of the Westminster Parliament. The modernisation process was aimed at restoring public confidence in politics by updating the institutions in which it is practised. As the Labour Government begins its third consecutive term in office, the Hansard Society believes that this is an appropriate moment to take stock of the nature, extent and overall impact of parliamentary modernisation in order to assess what has been achieved, what has not, and what should happen next.

Although our investigation focuses on the period between 1997 and 2005, it is not intended as a judgement of the Labour Government. For one thing, 1997 is not year-zero in terms of parliamentary reform; for, as Robin Cook noted during the course of this inquiry, 'in politics one never inherits a blank slate'. Indeed, the last years of John Major's Conservative Government saw the beginning of several reforms on which Labour was to build. This is, therefore, an investigation into the latest stage of what has been a longer voyage. But the period since 1997 may legitimately be viewed as a distinct phase on that journey and one during which considerable ground was covered. Moreover, it has also been a phase, according to some observers, when the traditional course of parliamentary reform may have been significantly altered.

In part, this is because, in the mid-1990s, Labour MPs began to employ the word 'modernisation' in the context of parliamentary reform. But modernisation means different things to different people. Tony Wright has observed that there are two principal meanings of 'modernisation', as applied to Parliament, which lead in different directions: 'First, there is the kind of modernisation favoured by governments (and many of their supporters)...the kind that wants to process business more efficiently and predictably, at more agreeable hours...Second, there is the kind of modernisation that wants to shift the existing balance between executive and legislature in significant respects, notably by strengthening

6

Parliament's scrutiny function' (2004: 869-70). The key issue when discussing the modernisation of Parliament, then, is modernisation to what end; or as Oonagh Gay puts it: 'fit for whose purpose?' (Gay 2005a).

Calls for reform of Parliament in the post-1997 period have, therefore, raised the question of what Labour meant by its pledge to 'modernise' Parliament. Although the party failed to produce any single policy document outlining its blueprint for a modern Parliament, a number of leading figures made several speeches in which they identified the core elements of their vision of modernisation. Ann Taylor gave an outline of Labour's plans for parliamentary reform in a speech delivered to Charter 88 one year before she became Commons Leader. Fashionably entitled 'New Politics, New Parliament', her speech emphasised that Labour saw the 'conventional reformist' agenda of altered sitting hours, better office accommodation and timetabling as 'not being essential to the main project of re-engaging the gears of the political process in a fundamental way so that ordinary voters feel genuinely connected with the people that represent them'. Instead, Taylor emphasised that a Labour Government would be primarily concerned with improving Parliament's capacity to produce better legislation by enabling MPs to more effectively hold the executive to account: 'Those tasks will be Labour's true project for Parliament and, awkward though it may appear to a few on our side, a more accountable Government is a better Government and ultimately a more re-electable Government' (Taylor 1996). Interestingly, Taylor asserted that it was not for the executive to dictate the programme of reforms: 'Parliament must own the process'. Subsequently, the Labour manifesto contained a pledge to set up a parliamentary select committee specifically charged with leading the process of modernisation.

This pledge was clearly linked to the Report of the Joint Consultative Committee on Constitutional Reform produced by the Labour Party and Liberal Democrats. In summer 1996 Tony Blair and Paddy Ashdown asked Robin Cook and Robert Maclennan to explore the possibility of co-operation between the parties in relation to constitutional reform. This led to the publication of a final report in 1997 in which the two parties committed themselves to working together in order to achieve a range of constitutional goals. The reform of Parliament formed a central aspect of this agreement and the report stated, 'The House of Commons no longer holds ministers to account and legislation is not given the scrutiny it requires' (Cook & Maclennan 2005). The parties' priorities for the House of Commons included: programming of parliamentary business; strengthening the ability of MPs to make government answerable for its actions; and, enhancing the role of select committees in ensuring the accountability of government departments.

By the time of the 1997 general election, it was therefore possible to identify three essential objectives that Labour sought to achieve through a programme of 'modernisation': firstly, it wanted to improve the operation and effectiveness of Parliament; secondly, it sought to shift the balance of power so that the legislature was better able to scrutinise and hold the executive to account; and thirdly, it wished to improve the image of Parliament in order to tackle the perceived problem of declining public confidence in the political process.

The study that follows seeks to assess the extent to which these three objectives have been realised by identifying changes to parliamentary procedure and practice since 1997. It then identifies a number of small but important and pragmatic reforms that should inform the future parliamentary modernisation agenda. The main focus of the inquiry is on the changes to the House of Commons, although as modernisation of the Commons affected the overall workings of Parliament, a number of changes to procedure and practice in the House of Lords are also given consideration. However, before examining the extent to which parliamentary modernisation has achieved the three broad objectives outlined in the introduction, it is first necessary to provide a brief overview of parliamentary developments over the last eight years to outline the context in which change took place and the factors that influenced the form, nature and pace of modernisation.

2 | Parliamentary modernisation since 1997: an overview

The energy and momentum behind Labour's commitment to modernising British democracy, displayed through its commitment to a wide-ranging programme of constitutional reform in the first years of the Government, led most observers to expect that measures to strengthen Parliament would be equally swift and momentous. Those in favour of Labour's promised modernisation of Parliament were therefore much encouraged by the establishment, almost immediately after the new Government was formed, of a Select Committee on the Modernisation of the House of Commons with a remit that included the duty to '...look at the means by which the House holds ministers to account'. The committee quickly got into its stride and in July 1997, just a few weeks after the general election, when most other select committees were still deciding on their future programme of work, published its first report on *The Legislative Process* (1997-98, HC 190). The report included proposals to introduce programme motions for the timetabling of Bills; pre-legislative scrutiny and draft Bills; flexible scrutiny of Bills; more explanatory notes on Bills; and the carry-over of public Bills into the following session (1997-98, HC 190). Many proposals were swiftly adopted and the parliamentary landscape significantly changed.

The first report on the legislative process was followed by others including *Explanatory Material for Bills, Carry-over of Public Bills* and *Scrutiny of European Business* (1997-98, HC 389; HC 543; HC 791). Ostensibly, therefore, it seemed to some that Ann Taylor – the new Leader of the House – was moving in the right direction towards achieving the ambitious aims of her 1996 'New Parliament' speech. Although no one could seriously claim that the relationship between Parliament and government had been refigured, or was even coming close to that, the Government had quickly set up a mechanism to deliver change and generally well-received proposals had emerged from its initial report on improving the legislative machinery of Parliament. Another early aspect of the modernisation programme was the formation of a Joint Committee on Parliamentary Privilege. The Committee undertook a review of parliamentary privilege and reported in April 1999, with a main proposal that there should be a Parliamentary

Privileges Act (1998-99, HC 43-I; HL 214-I). However, this proposal was not taken up and the Committee was subsequently disbanded.

Critics began to argue that the course of modernisation was being carefully steered away from one aimed at the redistribution of parliamentary power towards an agenda directed at securing smooth passage for the Government's legislative programme, which Ann Taylor had admitted was 'particularly heavy' (quoted in Seaton & Winetrobe 1999: 152). Such concerns hardened after July 1998 with the appointment of Margaret Beckett as Commons Leader. Peter Riddell has argued that Beckett adopted a party, rather than a parliamentary, view; an assessment supported by Paul Tyler, the former Liberal Democrat Shadow Leader of the House, who described her as an 'Old Labour' manager. Although Beckett introduced a number of significant modernising reforms, including the establishment of Westminster Hall as an additional debating chamber, it is generally agreed that the Government's commitment to strengthen Parliament substantially declined during her spell as Leader of the House.

It is questionable whether this slowing of place was down to Beckett's personal inclination or whether she was accurately reflecting a Cabinet position, and most specifically, the approach of Prime Minister Tony Blair. A number of participants to this study asserted that the Prime Minister does not take a keen interest in Parliament and, indeed, there has long been a general perception that Tony Blair has never been a 'Commons Man'. The modernisation process, in as much as it received Government backing, was focused on making Parliament more efficient and its ways of working more up-to-date, as opposed to ensuring that it is able to hold the government more rigorously to account. As will be discussed, when Robin Cook was publicly committed to genuine parliamentary reform, he received, at best, only lukewarm Cabinet backing. Although the notion that Tony Blair has no personal commitment to a stronger Parliament may not be entirely fair, nothing he has said on the subject has ever really dispelled that impression.

The change in stewardship from Ann Taylor to Margaret Beckett showed that having the Leader of the Commons as Chair of the Modernisation Committee was a double-edged sword (Gay 2005a). On the one hand, he or she could act as an enabling force – a powerful figurehead inside the

Cabinet arguing the case for reform and making it much more likely that the Committee's proposals would be accepted and implemented. On the other, the close involvement of a member of the executive, ultimately more concerned to guard the government than to strengthen Parliament, could see the Modernisation Committee diverted off an agenda of increasing accountability towards one concerned with improving parliamentary efficiency, and, perhaps consequently, to greater executive control.

By the end of the 1997-2001 Parliament, a number of MPs and parliamentary committees suggested that these concerns were justified. Perhaps most significant were the reports of the Liaison Committee, which consisted of the chairs of all the select committees. The Committee had traditionally tended to concentrate on the internal administration of select committees, but towards the end of the 1997 Parliament its work suggested that it was developing a higher profile on behalf of Parliament. In 2000, it published *Shifting the Balance: Select Committees and the Executive* (1999-2000, HC 300), which criticised the Government for not taking the issue of parliamentary scrutiny seriously enough and made a number of far-reaching recommendations that aimed to increase the power and role of the select committees vis-à-vis the executive. Although the Government rejected most of its proposals, (May 2000: c4737), the dismissive nature of its official response, described by one commentator as 'one of the most oily and evasive documents to emerge from Whitehall in recent years', merely served to stoke the fire of reform (Riddell 2003: 248).

The Liaison Committee responded by publishing a highly critical report – *Independence or Control?* (2000, HC 748) – in which it expressed frustration at the executive's attitude. In addition to the Liaison Committee's inquiries, two other reports looked specifically at the case for promoting the role of Parliament. In July 1999 the then Leader of the Conservative Party, William Hague, established a Commission on Strengthening Parliament, chaired by Lord Norton of Louth, whose remit was to 'examine the cause of the decline in the effectiveness of Parliament in holding the executive to account, and to make proposals for strong democratic control over the Government'. Two months later the Hansard Society established the Commission on Parliamentary Scrutiny, chaired by Lord Newton of Braintree. The Newton Report's executive summary emphasised: 'Despite recent innovations, particularly in the handling of legislation, the central question of Westminster's scrutiny of the executive has not been addressed'. The two commissions made a series of recommendations that dovetailed and together constituted a far-reaching agenda for change (see Norton 2000a; Hansard Society 2001).

Philip Norton (2000b: 13) has outlined how significant parliamentary reform demands a 'window of opportunity', and for such an opportunity to arise, three conditions must usually be fulfilled: a general election must recently have been held; a clear reform agenda must have been published providing a coherent set of proposals for MPs to unite behind; and, there has to be political leadership and commitment. In 2001, such a confluence arose. Labour won a second landslide general election victory, a coherent agenda for parliamentary reform began to crystallise out of the reports of various committees and commissions, and in June, Robin Cook was moved from the Foreign Office to become Leader of the House. Cook was widely viewed as a 'Commons Man' who would be sympathetic to moves to strengthen Parliament and improve its capacity to scrutinise legislation and hold the government to account. It was unfortunate, therefore, that the first major test of his stewardship was as a brazen example of (attempted) Government dominance over Parliament. The Government wanted to remove Donald Anderson and Gwyneth Dunwoody, both outspoken and respected select committee chairs, and replace them with chairs considered more in tune with Government thinking. There was open dissent within the Parliamentary Labour Party and the Government nominees were defeated in the subsequent Commons vote. For the first time, large numbers of Labour backbenchers demonstrated their willingness to assert their own, and Parliament's, authority vis-à-vis the executive. Their determination was shared by members of other parties, notably Kenneth Clarke, Gillian Shephard, Paul Tyler, and Sir George Young, who expressed their hopes for a stronger Parliament by joining the cross-party *Parliament First* group of MPs, chaired by former Labour minister Mark Fisher, which was formed in 2001. In the same year, an All-Party Group on Parliamentary Reform was established, chaired by Anne Campbell, which provided another non-partisan forum to promote change.

The Anderson/Dunwoody incident is seen by some as a turning point in the process of parliamentary modernisation, acting as the final straw for many MPs who had become disenchanted with the Beckett period of Commons Leadership and felt that Parliament was not doing its job properly in terms of holding the Government to account. Combined with concern at the dramatic drop in turnout in the 2001 general election, Robin Cook recognised that a 'window of opportunity' had opened in which Parliament could be significantly reformed. In his two years as Commons Leader, he successfully implemented a range of important parliamentary reforms first outlined in the Modernisation Committee report, *Modernisation of the House of Commons: A Reform Programme* (2001-02, HC 1168-1). It is important to recognise that Cook had to work extremely cleverly and assiduously to push through his reforms, many of which were passed with relatively small majorities in the Commons and frequently without strong Government support. Indeed, during this inquiry, a number of MPs observed that Cook came up against significant opposition within the Cabinet during his time as Commons Leader. That said, the most notable defeat for Cook – in the form of his proposal to change the way that members are appointed to select committees through the use of a panel of senior MPs – owed more to backbench misgivings than executive obstruction.

In the end, Cook's leadership of the House came to an abrupt end with his resignation over the Iraq War in March 2003. He was replaced, briefly, by John Reid, who was quickly followed by Peter Hain. Hain claimed to have 'inherited a very clear vision' of modernisation; although in practice most of his energy was directed at the engagement agenda, notably through the Modernisation Committee's inquiry *Connecting Parliament with the Public* (HC 368), rather than on efforts to shift the balance of power between Parliament and the executive. Indeed, Hain had the difficult task of trying to consolidate Cook's reforms, with partial success. It remains to be seen whether the modernisation programme implemented under Cook will survive fully intact in the long term.

*   *   *   *   *   *

The following three sections consider in more detail the changes, and sometimes absence of change, that have characterised Labour's approach to parliamentary modernisation. The first section looks at measures relating to legislative reform, examining developments such as programming, the use of pre-legislative scrutiny and the scrutiny of delegated legislation. The second section examines issues and reforms concerning the scrutiny and accountability work of Parliament; in particular, the impact of changes to the rules governing parliamentary questions and reform of the select committee system. The third section explores changes to the organisation of parliamentary business, such as the parliamentary calendar, the sitting week and day, and the rules governing the broadcasting of Parliament. It also looks at Parliament's attempts to improve its standing in the eyes of the public, notably its efforts to widen public access to, and engagement with, the institution. A final concluding chapter draws together these themes to provide an overall analysis of the modernisation of Parliament since 1997, and puts forward a number of proposals that would improve Parliament's effectiveness, its relationship with the executive and its connection with the public.

3 | Assessing parliamentary modernisation since 1997

(i) The legislative process

This section concentrates on developments in relation to the legislative process, which had been the subject of numerous calls for reform long before the election of the Labour Government in 1997. Foremost among those was the Hansard Society Commission chaired by Lord Rippon, whose report, *Making the Law*, was published in 1992. That report was followed by various reports from within Parliament, most notably by the Procedure Committee, which advocated changes to the legislative process. In the mid-1990s, the Conservative Government oversaw a number of innovations, including the publication of Bills in draft and informal moves towards the programming of legislation. However, it cannot be argued that Westminster's law making process was substantially changed during this period. It was, therefore, no surprise that legislative reform became an early priority of the Modernisation Committee.

In July 1997 its first report, *The Legislative Process* (1997-98, HC 190), contained a number of proposals that were to impact significantly on Parliament's law making procedures. The Committee decided not to take oral evidence during the course of its inquiry but to rely instead on evidence from written submissions and existing reports, in particular *Making the Law*. The report contained a number of sensible recommendations that, if properly implemented, would improve the legislative process. Thus the Government's reform programme in the legislative field started on a positive note and, moreover, benefited from cross-party support. As the following discussion will show, however, eight years on this consensus has evaporated and the initial pace of legislative change has substantially slowed.

Programming of legislation

Of all the changes to the legislative process made since 1997, perhaps the most far reaching, and certainly the most controversial, was programming (or timetabling) of legislation. Indeed, the

Procedure Committee has described the introduction of programming as 'the most significant change for some years in the way the House considers Bills' (2003-04, HC 325). Before 1998, there were two ways in which the House of Commons could timetable the various stages of a Bill. The first involved informal timetabling, when government and opposition business managers, and whips, through a system known as the 'usual channels', agreed a timetable for the passage of a particular piece of legislation (See Rush & Ettinghausen 2002). The second method involved 'guillotine' motions, which were instigated by the government to curtail the time spent on Bills. Since 1998, programme motions have been introduced into the House of Commons (but not the House of Lords) to specify the amount of time that will be spent on a Bill. Programme motions are moved after a Bill's Second Reading and outline the timetable for future stages in the Commons. Crucially, programme motions specify a date by which proceedings in a standing committee must be concluded. They also specify the number of days on the floor of the House reserved for the Report Stage and Third Reading, but do not specify the actual dates for those proceedings.

The idea of programming was not new. It had been proposed by the Procedure Committee in 1985 (1984-85, HC 49), in the 1992 Report of the Select Committee on Sittings of the House, known as 'The Jopling Report', (1991-92, HC 20) and in *Making the Law*. Between 1994 and 1995, the Conservative Government made some informal moves to introduce voluntary agreements on the time allocation for Bills in order to improve their scrutiny (See HC Deb 19/12/1994 c1458-1510; 1994-95, HC 491 and HC Deb 2/11/1995 c405-449), but did not formally enshrine any system of programming. Given the widespread nature of proposals for programming that had previously been put forward, and with the example already set in the final years of the Conservative Government, it is perhaps not surprising that one of the first actions of the Commons Modernisation Committee was to recommend the introduction of programming, which it described as 'more formal' than the usual channels but 'more flexible than the guillotine' (1997-98, HC 190). Similarly, given the cross-party nature of the bodies that had previously proposed such a move, it was not surprising that the initial proposals secured broad support across the Commons. This unanimity, however, was destined not to last. In truth, the opposition parties had never been hugely enthusiastic about programming but initially felt that it might at least bring more certainty to the legislative process and perhaps allow more time for developments such as pre-legislative scrutiny. In practice, however, programming has not worked out in the way that many had hoped.

It is possible to identify three distinct stages in the development of programming since its introduction. The first phase was characterised by consensus, and indeed the first programme motion, moved in January 1998 for the Scotland Bill, was hailed as the 'first ever all-party programme motion' (Cabinet Office Press Notice, 13/1/98). This phase essentially ended because the opposition parties grew increasingly unhappy with the way programming was working, coming to regard it as a mechanism that made it 'easier [for the Government] to get its legislative programme through the House, and, in so doing lessen[s], rather than encourage[s] proper and adequate scrutiny' (Cowley & Stuart 2001: 272). Although the number of programme motions increased, most particularly from the 2000-01 parliamentary session onwards, they were no longer consensual. Rather, the programme motions put forward by the Government were essentially carried by the votes of its own MPs against the wishes of the opposition.

Almost all government Bills are now programmed but the programme motions themselves are not generally debated. As far as critics of the system are concerned, programmes simply represent the government's decision on how long the committee stage should take and that the initial intention, that programming should represent the outcome of negotiations between parties, has been abandoned. The potential for consensus and discussion within programming committees was not realised and this aspect rapidly faded away. Furthermore, critics claim that programming has failed to enhance Parliament's scrutiny function, pointing to the large number of Bill clauses that are not being debated at all in Standing Committees. Reports from the Procedure and Modernisation Committees have attempted to address such concerns and have suggested ways that the operation of programming could be improved but, some modifications aside, the essential features of programming remain in place (Modernisation Committee 2002-03, HC 1222, Procedure Committee 2003-04, HC 325 and HC 1169).

Having been introduced in an atmosphere of general consensus, programming has become one of the most divisive issues in Parliament. Contributors to this study were therefore unsurprisingly contradictory in their assessments of its operation. From the Government perspective, Peter Hain believes that programming has improved the management of business and, moreover, has shifted power away from the executive by giving MPs greater awareness about when issues are likely to be on the agenda, in contrast to the previous system, which was completely opaque.

Mark Fisher, on the other hand, contends that while programming was sensible in principle, in practice it has weakened the opposition by depriving it of the potential 'time weapon' of delay and obstruction. He also believes that scrutiny has not, in any event, significantly improved. Tony Wright likewise believes that programming has worked out badly in practice and regards it as the 'guillotine by another name', with the result that many amendments do not get debated. Opposition members are even more trenchant in their criticism. Sir Nicholas Winterton described programming as a 'catastrophic disaster', while Sir Alan Haselhurst, a Deputy Speaker, was moved to comment on programming in the following terms (2001-02, HC 1168 Appendix 42):

It was difficult to escape the conclusion that a reform which had originally been proposed as a way of securing a fair balance between the interests of the government, the opposition and other sections of the House, and ensuring adequate consideration of all parts of each Bill had become just another weapon in the armoury for managing the business of the House.

It was hoped that programming would allow more effective and consistent scrutiny of proposed legislation while recognising both the need for the government to get its legislation through, and for the opposition to hold debates and votes on the parts of a Bill that it considered important. However, the breadth and depth of criticisms from across the political spectrum suggest that these hopes have not been realised. The disappointment of those who advocated reform of the system arises from the fact that programming has been detached from other reform proposals, most particularly the introduction of some form of Business Committee in the Commons. Such a committee would, proponents of the idea have long argued, deliver greater transparency and independence in the allocation of time for the legislative programme and, depending on the model of committee proposed, would also allow more equitable organisation on other aspects of parliamentary business. According to Oonagh Gay, 'The reformers had hoped for a Business Committee model, to allow more transparency and independence in the allocation of time. This was vetoed by the whips' (2005a citing 2001-02, HC 1168).

Numerous contributors to this study, among them Sir Nicholas Winterton, Mark Fisher and Paul Tyler, have identified the introduction of a Business Committee as the key to improving the way that the Commons organises its time and negotiates with government on the terms of its work. To date, there have been no formal moves to replace the opaque system of the 'usual channels' with a Business Committee. The closest move in this direction was during Robin Cook's reforms when it was decided that there would be increased consultation with the opposition parties on the broad shape of the coming legislative year. However, this change does not appear to have made much real difference to the way that business is organised. As Mark Fisher put it, no mechanism exists for Parliament to express itself and 'Government has Parliament in a stranglehold'. Although not all parliamentarians share this analysis, many believe the relationship between Parliament and government remains seriously unbalanced, having been tilted further in the wrong direction by the consequences of programming.

Pre-legislative scrutiny

Pre-legislative scrutiny represents another significant feature of the Labour Government's changes to the legislative process, albeit one, unlike programming, which is almost universally welcomed. Prior to a government Bill being formally published in final form, it may be published in draft. Since 1997, an increasing number of draft Bills have been referred to a parliamentary committee for pre-legislative scrutiny. Most draft Bills are referred to a Commons departmental select committee or a joint committee of both the Commons and the Lords for close consideration. The government will publish a list of Bills to be considered in pre-legislative form at the beginning of each parliamentary session. At present, only a relatively small (but growing) proportion of government Bills are subject to pre-legislative scrutiny. When considering legislation in draft form, select committees are able to call witnesses for oral evidence and take written evidence from external sources. Select committees are then able to report their findings in detail and explain why they support or oppose the proposed Bill and explain the amendments that they deem appropriate. The government is not obliged to accept the alterations from the committee, but in many cases it has done so. As well as considering particular provisions of a Bill, pre-legislative scrutiny can also consider the human rights implications, spending implications and delegated powers related to a Bill. Pre-legislative scrutiny can provide a forum for a wide range of interested and expert parties to influence legislation at an early stage, thus providing an important mechanism for collaboration between the executive, legislature and electorate. Most crucially, as ministers tend to commit less political capital to draft than to formal legislation, they do not necessarily regard making changes to a draft Bill as a defeat. It may even be considered more advantageous to ministers if their draft legislation is altered at this stage, to permit smoother passage in the formal legislative process.

As with programming the origins of pre-legislative scrutiny can be found in the latter years of the Conservative Government. However, whereas that administration issued some draft Bills for informal consultation, the Labour Government formally submitted draft Bills to committees for scrutiny, ensuring that, in essence, there was a new stage in Parliament's legislative process (at least, for those Bills chosen). The major step forward in the development of pre-legislative scrutiny came with the Modernisation Committee's report in 1997, which concluded:

There is almost universal agreement that pre-legislative scrutiny is right in principle, subject to the circumstances and nature of the legislation. It provides an opportunity for the House as a whole, for individual backbenchers, and for the opposition to have a real input into the form of the actual legislation which subsequently emerges, not least because ministers are likely to be far more receptive to suggestions for change before the Bill is actually published... Above all, it should lead to better legislation and less likelihood of subsequent amending legislation (1997-98, HC 190).

Since 1997, there has been a significant increase in pre-legislative scrutiny. Between the 1997-98 and 2003-04 parliamentary sessions a total of 42 draft Bills were published. The significant expansion in pre-legislative scrutiny came under Robin Cook's leadership of the House. The Modernisation Committee Report, *Modernisation of the House of Commons: A Reform Programme*, which outlined Cook's vision for reform, stated that 'we hope eventually to see publication in draft become the norm. We recommend that the Government continue to increase with each session the proportion of Bills published in draft' (2001-02, HC 224).

To help consolidate the process, in May 2002 the Commons adopted guidelines for core functions and duties to be carried out by select committees, including: 'to conduct scrutiny of any published draft Bill within the committee's responsibilities'. Extra resources were provided through the establishment of a Scrutiny Unit in November 2002 to assist with pre-legislative and financial scrutiny. Crucially, pre-legislative scrutiny has proved an effective means for increasing Parliament's capacity to influence and shape laws. For example, the Government accepted 120 of the 148 recommendations made by the joint committee looking at the draft Communications Bill in 2002. The Liaison Committee, in its Annual Report for 2004, drew attention to the increase in pre-legislative scrutiny being undertaken by select committees and highlighted a number of examples to indicate the impact that committees were making on the quality of legislation (2004-05, HC 419).

Nonetheless, questions remain about the extent of government control over the process. The decision of whether to publish a draft Bill, and to which committee it should be sent, is usually made at the discretion of the government. For example, the Work and Pensions Committee's request to examine the 2004 Pensions Bill in draft was declined on the grounds that the Government wanted to proceed immediately with a formal Bill (Riddell 2004). Conversely, it is possible for select committees to decline to undertake pre-legislative scrutiny on the grounds that they are over-burdened with work. Furthermore, there are no formal guidelines that indicate the sort of Bills that should be subject to pre-legislative scrutiny, or indicate whether a House of Commons select committee or a joint committee of both Houses should be chosen as the most appropriate forum for debate. Once again, the absence of a Business Committee is relevant as it could provide a forum for debate on issues such as which Bills should be subject to pre-legislative scrutiny.

Pre-legislative scrutiny has been widely welcomed. Tony Wright summed up the views of many parliamentarians interviewed for this study, saying that "Draft legislation would count as my big gain. The way legislation is considered is frequently the worst aspect of how Parliament operates. Pre-legislative scrutiny has improved that enormously." Many MPs and peers wish to see pre-legislative scrutiny expanded and the Government has given encouraging signs on this; Phil Woolas, then Deputy Leader of the House, stated that 'my view, and more importantly the Government's view, is that a Bill should be published in draft form unless there are good reasons for not doing so' (HC Deb 24/2/2004 c19 WH).

However, if pre-legislative scrutiny were more routinely used, there is a danger that select committees might become overloaded with work. Additionally, as the Liaison Committee pointed out, time constraints can hamper the effectiveness of pre-legislative scrutiny; for example, select committees have had difficulties in meeting government deadlines for its completion (2002-03, HC 558). There is a limit to what select committees are able to do, at least in the form that they are currently structured. The Hansard Society Commission report, *The Challenge for Parliament,* suggested several ways that select committees could be differently constituted. For example, the report proposed that they should have more members and that all backbench MPs should be expected to sit on a select committee. It also proposed that select committees should operate through a system of sub-committees to allow MPs to pursue different specialisations and interests. To recognise the expanded role of select committees, and the potential greater demands on MPs' time, the report proposed that there should be one day each week when the chamber did not sit to allow greater time for committees to meet. None of these proposals have, however, been adopted. Nonetheless, the potential dangers of overload aside, pre-legislative scrutiny has been one of the notable successes of parliamentary reform since 1997 and seems certain to remain a feature of parliamentary procedure in the future.

Carry-Over of Bills

Another major change has been the introduction of carry-over of Bills from one session to another, which was designed to mitigate the problems of a constrained and over-crowded parliamentary timetable. One of the main reasons given for introducing carry-over was to allow greater time for scrutiny of Bills, including pre-legislative scrutiny. According to Lord Norton:

> The case for carry-over is clear ... Allowing a Bill to carry-over from one session to another allows for the staggered introduction of Bills and for a more even distribution of parliamentary resources. It avoids what Robin Cook has characterised as the 'tidal wave' approach to legislation, ... It enables Parliament to give time for detailed scrutiny without having to be unnecessarily rushed to get through everything by the end of the session (Norton 2004).

Proposals for carry-over of Bills had been made for many years (e.g. *Making the Law* 1992) before being proposed in the Modernisation Committee's first report in 1997, and subsequently, in its 1998 report, *Carry-Over of Bills* (1997-98, HC 543). These reports recommended that, in certain defined circumstances, it should be possible to carry over a Bill to complete its remaining stages in the following session. The first Bill subject to carry-over was the Financial Services and Markets Bill in 1999 (see below). Once again it was Robin Cook's reforms that saw carry-over become more widely used. In 2002 both Houses made provision for the carry-over of some Bills from one session to another. In October 2004, motions were passed to confirm the procedures for use of carry-over for government Bills. In November 2004 the Government introduced the Gambling Bill at the end of the parliamentary session. As a result, most of its legislative stages were subsequently carried-over into the following session (thereby reversing the usual situation that only the latter stages of a Bill are carried-over).

There are some who assert that carry-over, once again, has advantaged the government over Parliament. They argue that the pressure to accede to amendments at the end of the session, to avoid a Bill from being lost, is reduced in cases where carry-over is possible. Nonetheless, carry-over commands broad support and looks likely to remain a lasting reform from this period.

The Financial Services and Markets Act: A case study

For those who allege that little has changed in Parliament in recent years and that its procedures have not been modernised, it is worth looking in some detail at the passage of the Financial Services and Markets Act 2000. There were many distinctive, and innovative, features of the Bill's passage, which, taken together, amounted to a radical departure from those which had gone before.

Before the Financial Services and Markets Bill was considered by Parliament, the Treasury published a draft Bill. The financial services industry, the public and three parliamentary committees were given the opportunity to comment on the draft legislation before it was put before Parliament. It was first examined by the House of Commons Treasury Select Committee (1998-99, HC 73-I), before becoming the first Bill to be considered in draft by a Joint Committee of both Houses of Parliament (1998-99, HC 328). It was the first significant piece of legislation which needed to be certified by ministers as compatible with the European Convention on Human Rights. Additionally, it was the first public Bill to be subject to the carry-over procedure, allowing its passage to span two parliamentary sessions (see Smith-Hughes 2001). The work of a joint committee of the Commons and the Lords, established specifically to scrutinise the draft legislation, was especially significant, holding seven oral evidence sessions and examining some 60 written submissions. Moreover, in being given a specific remit that included scrutinising the proposed arrangements for the accountability of the FSA, the Joint Committee was also able to examine options for the ongoing parliamentary scrutiny of the FSA. This procedure allowed concerns and practical issues to be raised and incorporated into the process.

Delegated legislation

Delegated legislation is one of the most important parts of the law but the procedures for its passage are one of the most neglected, and poorly regarded, aspects of the legislative process. Moreover, there is a clear distinction between the work of the Commons and the Lords. Indeed, the way that the two Houses scrutinise delegated legislation strengthens the case of those who assert that the Lords provide more rigorous scrutiny of legislation than the Commons.

In the past few decades there has been a massive growth in the use of delegated (or secondary) legislation. In 1970, Statutory Instruments filled 4,880 pages of legislation; by 1996 that had grown to 10,230 pages (1999-2000, HC 48). Such legislation provides much of the crucial powers and provisions not contained in primary legislation. The procedures for Parliament's consideration of delegated legislation have been severely and regularly criticised. For example, the Liaison Committee described the scrutiny of secondary legislation as 'woefully inadequate' (1999-2000, HC 300) and the Norton Commission described delegated legislation procedures as 'close to preposterous', arguing that major change is needed to existing arrangements (2000). Given this negative verdict it is not surprising that there have been calls for major reform of the system. In 1996 and 2000, dates which are significant as they fall under both Conservative and Labour administrations, the Commons Procedure Committee published two virtually identical reports on the subject (1995-96, HC 152; 1999-2000, HC 48). Both called for substantial improvements to the way that Parliament scrutinises delegated legislation. Given the weight of support for such proposals, it might have been reasonable to assume that this area would have been a priority for reform. In fact, only the House of Lords has made any real progress.

In 2003 the Lords established the Merits of Statutory Instruments Committee to serve as a sifting mechanism to identify those Statutory Instruments (SIs) that were important and merited further debate or consideration. The Committee considers every SI laid before Parliament and determines whether special attention should be drawn to them, on grounds such as whether it is politically or legally important or that it is inappropriate in view of the changed circumstance since the passage of the parent Act. To date, the Committee has produced numerous reports advising the House on the scrutiny of delegated legislation and has covered issues ranging from draft regional assembly and local government referendums, to horse passports and regulations concerning medicines for human use. Following the decision of the House of Lords to establish the Merits Committee, the Commons' Procedure Committee issued a further report in 2003, which concluded:

> We welcome the Lords' decision to appoint a sifting committee, but
> emphasise our view that it would be advantageous for discussions

to begin immediately with a view to establishing a Joint Committee for sifting delegated legislation from the outset. The alternative of waiting for the Lords' Committee to start and then attempting to join in later strikes us as much less sensible (2002-03, HC 50).

The Government rejected the Committee's proposals, claiming that, 'a sifting committee may lead to greatly increased demands on parliamentary time' (2002-03, HC 684). There was, however, one significant change to delegated legislation through the Regulatory Reform Act 2001, which was an extension of the Deregulation and Contracting Out Act 1994 and widened the provisions to cover burdens affecting individuals. However, this apart, the Government has not made any headway with reform to this crucial part of the legislative process and calls for reform will, no doubt, continue to be made.

Scrutiny of European Legislation

Most of the modernisation reforms concentrated on domestically initiated legislation. However, according to a Cabinet Office report in 2002, about 50 per cent of 'significant legalisation' enacted in the United Kingdom originates in Europe. Despite the volume of new law coming from Europe, the procedures for authorising and scrutinising it attract little interest and are not well understood. Nonetheless, as the Hansard Society Commission on Parliamentary Scrutiny noted in 2001, 'the two Houses [of Parliament] provide the UK with some of the most effective parliamentary scrutiny of European matters of any of the 15 member states'.

The scrutiny of European Union issues is a good example of the two Houses of Parliament working in a complementary and mutually beneficial manner. The House of Lords' European Union Committee operates with a number of sub-committees involving some 70 peers and carries out detailed scrutiny of proposed EU legislation. It looks at a relatively small number of areas in considerable detail (about 40-50 each year) and takes a different approach to that of the Commons' European Scrutiny Committee, which rapidly sifts all proposals under consideration in the Council of Ministers (usually about 400 a year). These arrangements are supplemented by the European Scrutiny Reserve, a resolution of the House of Commons that UK ministers should not enter into any new commitment in the Council of Ministers until scrutiny in the Commons has been completed (apart from in exceptional circumstances). A similar resolution applies to the House of Lords.

The Modernisation Committee inquired into European Scrutiny in 1998 (1997-98, HC 791) and its proposals were implemented in November 1998. The measures included strengthening the scrutiny reserve resolutions by bringing in other areas of European competence (such as joint decisions and strategies as allowed under the Treaty of Amsterdam), extending powers to scrutinise legislation on issues such as Foreign and Security Policy and introducing greater monitoring of the Council of Ministers by the European Scrutiny Committee.

Although the reforms introduced in 1998 strengthened the European scrutiny system, by 2004 calls for further improvement were again being made. Responding to criticism from the Confederation of British Industry, that MPs are 'asleep on the job' about European legislation, Peter Hain conceded that there was a tendency for the 'average' parliamentarian to ignore EU rules and that individual MPs needed to 'up their game' to improve parliamentary scrutiny of European legislation. Nonetheless, Hain believed that 'The European Scrutiny Committee does an excellent job sifting through these piles of documents that come from Brussels but they do not mainstream the issue' (interview with BBC Radio 4's *Today* programme, 20 August 2004). He said that tighter scrutiny of Brussels was a key issue being looked at as part of the House of Commons' modernisation agenda, and that a new parliamentary committee was to be set up to improve the scrutiny of EU legislative proposals which would enable MPs to examine and influence such measures at an earlier stage. This committee is expected to take public evidence from government ministers, MEPs and EU Commissioners. However, Gwyneth Dunwoody questioned whether it was constitutionally legitimate to allow MEPs and other members of European institutions to be scrutinised at Westminster.

In March 2005, the Modernisation Committee published its report, *Scrutiny of European Business* which contained many recommendations to improve the way that Westminster scrutinises the legislation and activities of the European Union (2004-05, HC 465-I). These recommendations included the establishment of a new Joint Grand

Committee to consider European Union matters, which, as indicated in the above interview, would be able to take evidence from a European Commissioner, and also proposed reforms to improve the effectiveness of the European Scrutiny Committee. Coming so close to the date of the General Election, the report set the agenda for European scrutiny in the new Parliament.

The Joint Committee on Human Rights

Although not formally part of the modernisation process, the passing in 1998 of the Human Rights Act, and the incorporation of the European Convention on Human Rights into UK law, has had a significant impact on the legislative process. The Act required the UK courts to interpret and give effect to the laws made by Parliament, as far as possible, in a way which is compatible with the rights guaranteed in the Convention. In the wake of this major constitutional development, a Joint Committee on Human Rights (JCHR) was established in January 2001 with a remit to consider and report on matters relating to human rights in the United Kingdom (but specifically excluding consideration of individual cases) and, in particular, to carry out proactive scrutiny of proposed primary and secondary legislation for human rights compatibility. This development was particularly notable as being the first permanent Joint Committee of both Houses. Since its formation, the Committee has looked at every Bill introduced into either House; in total it has examined well over 300 Bills and has drawn the special attention of each House to around 100 of these. Sometimes its reports have drawn Parliament's attention to relatively minor concerns about compliance, while others have gone to the heart of a Bill's purpose (Evans 2004).

According to Paul Evans, former clerk to the Committee, one of the JCHR's main effects has been to increase awareness within government departments that every Bill will be examined: 'It is the *threat* of unavoidable, detailed and well-supported parliamentary scrutiny that is the key factor here in enhancing Parliament's influence on legislative outcomes' (2004). Furthermore the Committee has had some success in persuading departments to give a fuller account of the Convention rights issues which they believe are engaged by particular provisions. In this, it is trying to engender a *culture of justification* within government, rather than allowing simply the tradition of assertion.

A particularly notable example of the innovative nature of the Committee's work took place in 2004 with its report on the meaning of 'public authority' under the Human Rights Act (2003-04 HL 39, HC 382). This was a highly unusual, perhaps unprecedented, example of Parliament taking on the courts over their interpretation of its intention in making law. The Committee showed that it was prepared to undertake a form of monitoring of what happens after legislation has been made and indicated the Committee's belief that the Human Rights Act required a different type of monitoring. By establishing such a Committee, Parliament has provided a certain counterweight to the government and the courts on this issue and has shown itself able to adapt effectively to new developments. Over the longer term, it may be that changes brought about by the incorporation of the Human Rights Act will come to be seen as among the most profound constitutional reforms of this period.

Legislative Reform: A mixed verdict

Westminster's legislative process is markedly different to the one inherited by the incoming Labour Government in 1997. The changes that have been implemented stand as a tangible correction to those who assert, wrongly, that Westminster is a fossilised institution, unable or unwilling to adapt itself to changed circumstances. Understandably, the modernisation process is of little interest to the population at large but, nonetheless, Parliament deserves more credit than it usually receives for making its procedures, in certain respects, more effective.

Many reforms since 1997 have been beneficial to Parliament, in terms of increasing its ability to scrutinise legislation. Innovations such as the increased use of draft Bills and pre-legislative scrutiny have been widely welcomed, enhancing the role and effectiveness of Parliament and enabling both parliamentarians as well as those outside Westminster to engage in the legislative process in a more meaningful way. Explanatory notes to accompany Bills mean that the provisions involved, and their purpose and implications, are more easily understood. The ability to carry-over Bills from one session to the next is a sensible innovation to allow greater time to scrutinise legislation and, potentially, to even out the more eccentric features of the parliamentary timetable. The example of the Financial Services and Markets Act, which is just one among many, shows the benefits of reform and how much has been achieved.

The use of joint committees consisting of members of both the Commons and Lords has increased and is a welcome development. Such committees consider draft Bills on a temporary basis and human rights on a permanent basis. The complementary functions of the two Houses are most apparent in relation to scrutiny of European issues and represents a model upon which Parliament should build.

Nevertheless, there is another side to this story. For example, the verdict on programming of legislation is much more complicated, ranging from pragmatic acceptance to outright hostility. The introduction of programming was advocated for many years by MPs from across the political spectrum, and few commentators wish to return to a totally unprogrammed system. It is evident that programming has brought some order and certainty to the legislative system. However, a strong case has been made, and not just by the opposition parties, that this greater certainty has been most beneficial to the government and further strengthened its dominance over the legislature. In the view of many observers, the reason why programming has attracted such controversy is because it has become detached from other reforms. Most reports that have advocated programming envisaged that it would be implemented in conjunction with the establishment of some form of Business Committee or Legislation Steering Committee. *Making the Law*, for example, made the case that programming would be a means to a greater end; namely, improved methods of scrutiny, which would be organised more consensually through a Business Committee. Such a committee would also allow the different parties, and backbench and frontbench interests, to have a role in organisation of the parliamentary timetable and the legislative process. Yet it is clear that the prospect of securing a Business Committee is inextricably linked to the executive's desire to maintain control. It would seem, therefore, that the Government has only been prepared to make changes that it found acceptable. As such, the reforms that it introduced were often disjointed and lacking coherence. In consequence, programming has not delivered all the benefits that its many proponents would have hoped.

Praise for the positive changes therefore has to be tempered by criticism of the inaction in other aspects of the process. These areas include the system of Private Members' Bills, which should provide individual parliamentarians with a more effective opportunity to develop their legislative function. In fact, private members procedures are quite clearly dominated by the interests of the executive, so much so that some commentators argue that they simply represent a sub-specie of government Bill. Standing committees, in the opinion of virtually all those who have close experience of them, do not perform well their role of scrutinising legislation and should be reformed. The scrutiny of delegated legislation has been widely criticised, particularly in the Commons, and is long overdue for reform. The growth of European Union legislation has had enormous impact on the British legislative process, to which Parliament has not yet adequately responded. These defects mean that pressure for reform remains very much alive. Significantly, the House of Lords Constitution Committee recently published a wide-ranging report into the way that Parliament considers legislation and put forward a comprehensive range of proposals for improvement (2003-04 HL 173-1).

More broadly, the Government can be criticised for not considering more fundamental and far-reaching changes to the way that Parliament makes the law. The amount of legislation, and the time and resources that Parliament has to scrutinise and authorise such a volume, attracts regular criticism. It was as long ago as 1947 that L.S. Amery, in *Thoughts on the Constitution*, argued that 'Parliament has become an overworked legislation factory'. Almost 60 years later, Sir Nicholas Winterton argued that Parliament suffers from 'grave indigestion and constipation' with far too much legislation stretching MPs, peers and their committees beyond their limit.

Yet there has been little debate about the totality and scope of the annual legislative programme. There has been little consideration of alternative models, such as greater use of Special Standing Committees, which would allow for expert witnesses to be called and which provide an additional forum for consideration and scrutiny. There have been no moves to experiment with dual-purpose committees, which combine standing and select committee functions. Such combined committees are the norm in many other Parliaments, including the Scottish Parliament and most of Western Europe, and their use might improve both the quality of legislation and accountability. As a whole, there has been little progress on the bigger picture of Parliament's law making functions.

Perhaps the main reason why the Government, and indeed any government, may be reluctant to consider fundamental change is that law making is neither an administrative process nor one that lends itself, naturally, to a high-minded and dispassionate approach (although any efforts to promote such qualities would surely be welcome). Instead, the system, as with everything to do with Parliament and government, is essentially political. Much of what happens has to be viewed through the prism of the political battle, the exercise of the mandate and pursuit and retention of power. The system we have essentially allows the government to get its legislation through in the form that it desires. There is, therefore, little incentive to change the basic underpinnings of the system. Viewed from that perspective, the Labour Government since 1997 has actually delivered a considerable number of beneficial reforms to the legislative process. In October 2004, the House of Commons voted to make permanent many of the legislative process reforms introduced since 1997, (including programming and the carry-over of government Bills), thus ensuring that this period would be characterised by lasting change (HC Deb 26/10/2004 c1273).

Given the political imperative and the government's dominant role in the system, reforms are best pitched as delivering something for both Parliament and government. Pre-legislative scrutiny, for example, can be viewed as a way of delivering greater efficiency for the government, allowing its proposals to be tested and scrutinised before it has committed itself to a final version. Similarly, proposals for post-legislative scrutiny, which have been made consistently but without much success, would, if implemented, allow for more rational appraisal of legislation and might appeal on grounds of efficiency and good governance.

Furthermore, many aspects of the legislative process are hidden from view. For example, Joan Ruddock pointed out how much influence Labour backbenchers have behind the scenes. Their access to ministers, she believed, makes a real difference to what is finally presented to Parliament. The same situation existed, one could suppose, when the Conservative Government was in power and so is a crucial determinant in the relationship between the executive and the legislature (or at least one part of the legislature). It is equally important to remember that the government must also deal with rebellions and dissent, which increased significantly in recent years (Cowley & Stuart 2005). It is inevitable that reforms to the legislative process, driven and controlled by the government as they inevitably are in the British political system, are seen in that realistic political light.

This section has looked at the procedures Parliament uses in making the law and at the various changes, or sometimes absence of change, that have occurred in this sphere. One central aspect of the process is the scrutiny given to the government's legislative proposals. The following section looks at a very different element of Parliament's scrutiny function: that of ensuring the accountability of the executive.

(ii) Parliamentary scrutiny of the executive

In this chapter, we consider a number of specific elements related to the way that Parliament scrutinises government and holds it to account for its actions. These elements include issues of ministerial and prime ministerial accountability; the role and function of select committees; Parliamentary Questions and the provision of information; as well as the impact of Freedom of Information legislation and questions of commercial confidentiality. In looking at these issues and the attempts to achieve reform in these areas, the chapter illuminates the core tension inherent in the relationship between Parliament and government – namely, the balance of power between the two. It is this tension that helps to explain the general, and at times contradictory, direction of the overall modernisation process.

The groundswell for radical reform

One key aspect of Labour's programme of parliamentary modernisation was a commitment to strengthen Parliament's ability to scrutinise government and increase ministerial accountability. Yet, for much of the period after 1997, little headway was made in that direction. Much work was done to reform the legislative process and likewise, as will be seen, considerable attention was given to measures aimed at updating Parliament's public image and improving its communicative capacity. But a glance at the Modernisation Committee's work over the last eight years (see Appendix 2) illustrates that, at least for the duration of the 1997 Parliament, its focus was generally on legislative and procedural issues, timetabling and the upgrading of media facilities, rather than the more fundamental matter of shifting power back to the legislature. Indeed, by the end of the 1997-2001 Parliament, MPs from across the political spectrum argued that if the scales had moved it was because they had tilted in the executive's favour (e.g. Wright 1999; Tyrie 2000; 2003; Tyler 2003).

The frustration created by the Government's refusal to undertake far-reaching parliamentary reform during its first term, augmented by a perception that Labour ministers were not treating Parliament with the respect it deserved, eventually found vent in the Liaison Committee's report, *Shifting the Balance: Select Committees and the Executive*

(1999-2000, HC 300). The Government's subsequent rejection of virtually every recommendation that the report proposed (see c4737) did little to assuage the mood of discontented backbenchers, still less the Liaison Committee, which followed its initial report with another in July 2000, *Independence or Control?* (2000, HC 748), in which it warned the Government that Parliament should not be taken for granted. It followed that in March 2001 with the publication of *Shifting the Balance – Unfinished Business* (2001, HC 321), which repeated the case for the reform package that had been outlined in the Liaison Committee's two previous reports. It also underlined the widespread support for parliamentary reform that was growing amongst backbench MPs, as evidenced three months later by the formation of *Parliament First* – a cross party grouping that aimed to promote the interests and influence of Parliament and to achieve a more balanced relationship with the executive. This reflected a wider trend, which Cowley and Stuart (2003; 2004) have documented, that saw MPs – particularly those on the Labour side – exercise greater independence of action and a willingness to rebel against the party line.

As noted earlier, the pressure for change was further bolstered by two important commissions – chaired by Lords Norton and Newton respectively – which had been set up around that time. The proposals in these two reports won support from a cross-section of external observers and dovetailed with recommendations contained within the reports of the Liaison Committee. For example, the Liaison Committee suggested in its March 2000 (HC 300) report that: the role of the whips in determining the membership of select committees should be curtailed; that an alternative career structure to ministerial office be established through the introduction of additional payments to select committee chairs; and, that committee resources should be increased and a new support unit be created within the Committee Office.

The agenda for change that began to form out of these proposals coincided with Labour's second landslide victory in the 2001 general election, and the appointment of a senior and reform minded Government figure, Robin Cook, as Leader of the House. The confluence of these three factors created a window of opportunity for the fundamental restructuring of Parliament, although it did not immediately appear so at the time. On 11 July 2001 the Committee of Selection announced the select committee memberships for the current Parliament. The composition of the proposed committees, particularly the removal of Gwyneth Dunwoody and Donald Anderson from the Transport and Foreign Affairs Committees respectively, aroused controversy. The following week, in a calculated display of defiance, over 100 Labour MPs voted against the Government to reject the proposed memberships of the Transport and Foreign Affairs Committees. This incident was important at three levels. First, it demonstrated the power of the executive, via the whips, in appointing members to Parliament's scrutiny committees. Second, it displayed the rather facile role of the Committee of Selection and consequently fuelled demands for severing the link between the executive and appointments to select committees. Finally, and most importantly, the incident revealed the latent power of Parliament.

Cook's radical agenda

The new Leader of the House, Robin Cook, distanced himself from any involvement in the affair but quickly announced a raft of reforms and reviews. Standing Orders were amended to give every select committee the freedom to decide for itself whether to appoint a sub-committee and the right to appoint a joint committee with other select committees. He also signalled his willingness to consider the proposals put forward by the Liaison Committee, Norton Commission and the Newton Commission to reduce the role of the whips and pay select committee chairs an additional salary in order to create an alternative career path to ministerial office within the House (Cook 2001a).

During the first three months of the 2001-2002 session the Modernisation Committee collected evidence from a large number of proponents of parliamentary reform, including Lords Newton and Norton. In December 2001 Robin Cook published a memorandum via the Modernisation Committee in which he set out his perspective on reform (HC 440). It was clear from the memorandum that Cook's interpretation of 'modernisation' was significantly different from those held by previous Leaders of the House since May 1997. There was a clear shift in emphasis away from Parliament's role as a legislature and towards its scrutiny function – 'Good scrutiny makes for good government' (para.2). The powers of select committees now formed the central focus of the Modernisation Committee's work, which involved an examination of the appointments process, resources and powers available to committees and the ability to take committee reports to the floor of the House. The memorandum formed a statement of purpose around which the wider debate about parliamentary reform could be based and the future work of the Modernisation Committee focused. Indeed, in February 2002 the Conservative Party published a policy paper, *Delivering a Stronger Parliament*, which broadly welcomed the Cook memorandum in addition to advocating the strengthening of select committees with new formal powers.

In line with the shift of focus signalled in the Cook memorandum, the Modernisation Committee published its first full report of the new Parliament, *Select Committees*, in February 2002 (HC 224). The report's recommendations were 'intended to enable Members of the House to be more effective in discharging their role of scrutiny' and were clearly influenced by the previous work of the Liaison Committee, and the Newton and Norton Reports. The recommendations fell into four main categories: appointments; resources; remit; and payment.

Reforms to select committees

Of central importance was the Modernisation Committee's return to the issue of nominations to select committees and the role of the whips. The controversy surrounding the initial committee memberships in July 2001 augmented the feeling that reform was necessary and cemented cross-party support in the debates in the House on 16 and 19 July 2001. The Modernisation Committee endorsed the comment of Lord Sheldon that 'the executive, via the whips, ought not to select those members of the select committees who will be examining the executive, that is crucial' (2001-02, HC 224).

The Modernisation Committee recommended that the Chairman of Ways and Means should chair a new Committee of Nomination whose members would be drawn predominantly from the Chairmen's Panel, which is itself appointed by the Speaker of the House of Commons. The proposed Committee of Nomination would have consisted of nine members (in addition to the non-voting Chairman of Ways and Means) drawn predominantly from the Chairmen's Panel (HC 224 paras. 7-23). The proposals therefore sought to respond to the criticism that the

Liaison Committee's 2000 (HC 300) recommendation for a three member Panel of Selection was too narrow. The Committee of Nomination would receive nominations from political parties in the same way as previously and then the final lists would be agreed through a vote in the House. The perceived value of the proposals was that a new Committee of Nomination would act as a counterweight to the executive in determining the composition of select committees.

The Modernisation Committee went on to endorse the previous recommendation of the Liaison Committee: that a central unit be established containing specialised staff with the expertise to support select committees in their scrutiny of the executive. It also recommended that the resources of the National Audit Office be more equitably shared amongst the select committees and that sufficient administrative staff should be made available to committees in light of their increasing duties and responsibilities. The increase in resources was seen as vital to achieving more systematic scrutiny of governmental activity. The growth in the size and responsibilities of the state coupled with the adoption of new forms of governance involving a mix of service providers, many of which enjoyed an arm's-length relationship with ministers, had not been matched by an increase in the scrutiny capacity of Parliament. Select committees have always prized their discretion to decide on the topics and issues deserving inquiry and have traditionally reacted against proposals that would impinge or impose structure on this freedom. However, during the previous Parliament the Liaison Committee had agreed that in future all select committees should publish annual reports on their activity so that common challenges and issues could be identified and addressed, as well as spreading examples of good practice. The Modernisation Committee recommended that an agreed statement would outline the core tasks of select committees (HC 224 paras. 31-35). The list of core tasks would then form the framework around which each select committee would structure their annual report. The aim of this recommendation was not to reduce the freedom of select committees but to encourage committees to broaden the scope of their work and develop a degree of consistency.

The final theme of the *Select Committees* report by the Modernisation Committee in February 2002 took on the proposal first suggested by the Liaison Committee in its *Shifting the Balance* report of March 2000 (HC

300), and subsequently supported in the Norton and Newton Commissions that the chairs of select committees should be paid an additional salary in recognition of the extra workload involved and to create an alternative parliamentary career structure to ministerial office. The Modernisation Committee recommended 'that the value of a parliamentary career devoted to scrutiny should be recognised by an additional salary to the chair of the principal investigative committees' (HC 224 para. 41).

Within weeks of the publication of the Modernisation Committee's report on select committees the Liaison Committee published its own report – *Select Committees: Modernisation Proposals* (HC 692) – which proposed many of the same recommendations, though not all. The Liaison Committee did not support the Modernisation Committee's recommendations to rename select committees 'scrutiny committees', increase the number of select committee members from 11 to 15 or impose a two-Parliament rule for chairs, but did endorse its recommendations regarding appointments, remit, resources and payment.

Prime Minister's appearance before the Liaison Committee

The parliamentary reform agenda received an unexpected boost in April 2002 when the Prime Minister wrote to the Chair of the Liaison Committee offering to appear twice a year before the committee (2001-02, HC 984). Attempts by the Public Administration Select Committee (PASC) and the Liaison Committee in the previous Parliament to secure the attendance of the Prime Minister had been unsuccessful (see 2000-01, HC 235; HC 321). The first session with the Prime Minister took place on 16 July 2002 and a regular pattern of twice-annual appearances has now been established (see 2001-02, HC 1095; 2002-03, HC 334; 2003-04, HC 310). The regular appearance of the Prime Minister before the Liaison Committee has undoubtedly filled a major gap in parliamentary scrutiny.

The format of the sessions has evolved and matured rapidly as an unwieldy collection of around 33 committee chairs (including domestic committee chairs) have had to find an acceptable way to structure the questioning. The procedure established towards the end of the 2001-2005 Parliament involves the Liaison Committee informing the Prime Minister and the media of the three main themes and issues that the committee would like to cover at the forthcoming session. But neither the

Prime Minister nor the Chair of the Committee is made aware of the specific questions in advance of the session. The nature of the questions and the level of reply given tend to allow a more constructive, informative and non-partisan dialogue than the theatrical and confrontational exchanges which typify Prime Minister's Questions in the chamber. The length of questioning, some two-and-a-half hours as compared to Prime Minister's Questions (PMQs) of 30 minutes, also provides an opportunity to examine an issue in some detail – with the Prime Minister on occasion agreeing to send the Liaison Committee a memorandum or further information.

However, while the working arrangements of the sessions have attempted to balance breadth and depth there is a limit to the number of issues that can be examined in each session. More broadly, twice-yearly appearances by the Prime Minister before the Liaison Committee should not become a constitutional veneer that seeks to mask or distract attention from the challenges faced by departmental select committees in their day-to-day scrutiny of the government and wider state. It is also important to recognise that it was the Prime Minister who decided to appear before the Liaison Committee. Parliament had previously failed to secure his attendance and had been unable to generate sufficient pressure to force an appearance. Despite this, the Prime Minister's decision to instigate regular appearances before the Liaison Committee marked a positive development for parliamentary scrutiny.

However, the buoyant mood of reformers was deflated to some extent after the Modernisation Committee's proposals received an unexpected setback in May 2002 when the plans for a new Committee of Nomination were rejected on an ostensibly free vote by 209 votes to 195. As Peter Hennessy (2004) noted bitterly, '...this was a case of kissing-the-chains-that-bind which quite took one's breath away – quite the lowest moment for select committees on the road from 1979. May 2002 really was the poverty of aspirations at its malign worst'. The Chair of the PASC, Tony Wright, similarly noted (2004: 870),

It should never be forgotten by those who parrot the glories of parliamentary sovereignty, or denounce wicked governments for blocking reforms to strengthen Parliament, that when a Leader of the House provided MPs with an opportunity to decide on a free vote whether they wanted the composition and chairs of select committees chosen by the whips and the party machines (as they are at present) or by themselves, they voted for the former option. This is more revealing about the real obstacles to serious reform than innumerable texts on the subject or routine polemics on the tyranny of the executive.

The Commons did, however, support the motion to introduce an additional salary for select committee chairs. It has been suggested that the introduction of additional payments (without the concomitant reforms to reduce the power of the whips) may actually have increased the executive's influence within the House by creating an additional tier of attractive patronage appointments. The Modernisation Committee had been aware of this possibility and had warned in its February 2002 report, 'It would be wholly unacceptable if paid chairmanships were to become an extension of political patronage' (HC 224 para.26) and yet, in essence, this is exactly what has happened.

Other more positive changes were agreed that might well increase the effectiveness of parliamentary scrutiny. These included the establishment of a set of common objectives (see Table 4), agreement for a new staffing unit to offer select committees more resources in financial scrutiny (bolstered by secondments from the National Audit Office). A new term limit for chairs was introduced, of two Parliaments or eight years, whichever is greater. Committees were also given the power to exchange papers with the Scottish Parliament and Welsh Assembly, thereby enhancing the potential for joint-working.

The May 2002 debate on parliamentary modernisation provided a classic example of the true balance of power within the House of Commons as well as an instructive insight into the Government's mentality since May 1997. From one perspective the debate and the subsequent votes illustrated that Robin Cook lacked the full support of the Prime Minister and his Cabinet colleagues in pushing forward his agenda. No member of the Cabinet voted with the Leader of the House. A second perspective illuminates the power and role of the whips. Although the modernisation proposals were tabled as a free vote in reality both the Conservative and Labour whips used every weapon in their arsenal to ensure that the proposal to create a new Committee of

Nomination was not supported. The role of the whips in orchestrating the executive's large majority against a proposal supported by the Liaison Committee, Modernisation Committee and the *Parliament First* cross-party group of MPs would seem to support the broader concern that the Labour Government has been committed to shifting the balance in *principle* but not in *practice* (see Gregory 1999). However, without a clear shift in the executive mentality to one that views parliamentary scrutiny not as a threat but as a vital component of good governance in a modern democracy, the modernisation reforms that were approved are likely to have a restricted impact.

The establishment of an agreed set of core tasks for select committees is a positive development, with the potential of enhancing the standard of parliamentary scrutiny (see Appendix 4), but is compromised by the realities of the balance of power within the House which effectively mean that select committees are *de facto* heavily reliant on the co-operation of ministers and civil servants. Without a shift in executive mentality select committees will gain very little from having their core tasks and duties codified. For example, Task 8 encourages select committees 'To scrutinise major appointments made by the department'. This task would appear to complement the Government's 1998 invitation in *Quangos – Opening Up Appointments* for select committees to play a greater role in the appointments process and the inclusion of this task was clearly fuelled by the perceived success of the Treasury Committee in relation to appointments to the Monetary Policy Committee. However, other committees have been less successful. Numerous committee annual reports complain of departmental and ministerial obstruction. In 2002, for example, the Education and Skills Committee and the Home Affairs Committee both reported that they had sought an active role in relation to specific senior appointments, that of HM Chief Inspector of Schools and the Chair of the Independent Police Complaints Commission, respectively. Both committees made recommendations to this effect, which were in both cases rejected by the Government.

However, the value of the core tasks is that they at least encourage select committees to reflect on the scope of their responsibilities and dedicate at least some time and resources to the scrutiny of issues and areas of government that may otherwise have been overlooked. The production of annual reports not only augments this pressure to expand committee activity but the review of all these annual reports by the Liaison Committee (see 2001-02, HC 590; 2002-03, HC 558; 2003-04, HC 446; 2004-2005, HC 419) may eventually force the Government, either formally or informally, to alter its stance.

In conducting their core tasks select committees are limited by a continued dearth of resources. Therefore, the creation of a Scrutiny Unit within the Committee Office of the House of Commons undoubtedly represents a positive development. However, the size and scope of the Scrutiny Unit is at present restricted. The unit consists of just 16 staff who are expected to support around 22 select committees and a number of joint committees in the scrutiny of expenditure and draft legislation. One committee chair noted that the Scrutiny Unit was simply 'spread too thin' to make any significant difference. The chair of the Transport Committee, Gwyneth Dunwoody, echoed this position when she noted that her committee is supported by just seven staff but is charged with overseeing a department of some 20,000 civil servants and public servants spread across the central department, seven executive agencies (e.g. Highways Agency), public corporations (e.g. Civil Aviation Authority), executive non-departmental public bodies (e.g. Strategic Railway Authority) and Public Interest Companies (e.g. Network Rail).

It is also important to recognise, as the Newton Commission emphasised (2001: 200), that parliamentary scrutiny is still predominantly based around ministerial departments and has not evolved to recognise that the vast majority of modern governance is exercised not by ministers in Whitehall departments but by appointed officials in so-called quangos and a range of other bodies. The reports of the Public Administration Select Committee have clearly illustrated the growing role and powers of these quasi-autonomous bodies (see 1998-99, HC 209; 2001-02, HC 367). Task 7 – 'To monitor the work of the department's Executive agencies, NDPBs, regulators and other associated public bodies' – therefore fulfils an important role in making select committees aware of the existence of these bodies. Since 2001 a number of committees, notably the Northern Ireland Affairs Committee, Health Committee and Treasury Committee, have employed their new powers to create sub-committees as a useful method for increasing the breadth of scrutiny. Indeed, according to the Sessional Returns for

1999-2000 to 2003-04, the use of sub-committees almost quadrupled between 1999 and 2003 (see Appendix 11).

Nonetheless, overall select committees still lack the time, expertise and resources to scrutinise more than a handful of the largest arm's length bodies. Indeed, the views of the majority of select committee chairs reflect a mixture of institutional apathy and political realism. The Chair of the Agriculture Committee (1999, HC 209: 162) noted:

> I'm afraid that there simply is not time for select committees to look at each and every one of the quangos within their remit...select committees simply do not have the time and resources to do what they already do, never mind having their burdens added to. I regard this as disappointing but an acceptance of reality.

It would, however, be wrong to assume that the scope and standard of parliamentary scrutiny could be improved simply through the provision of more staff and resources to select committees, whose members have frequently argued against an increase in resources for fear that their work may become staff-led. The central resource that a large number of interviewees suggested Parliament really needed was political will – rather than money or staff. Select committees already have expansive powers to demand 'persons, papers and records' but what they lack are members who are willing to use these powers. Parliamentary reform remains, at base, a cultural challenge and requires MPs to see it through.

The Newton Commission of 2001 stressed the importance of promoting a 'Scrutiny Culture' in which the loyalty of backbenchers should be balanced between the House, their constituents as well as party. During the 2001-2005 Parliament the culture of the House of Commons did evolve in a manner that was less compliant to the will of the executive, as demonstrated in the votes over tuition fees and foundation hospitals. This shift in culture created a pressure on the executive to respond and implement reforms that would vent this force and respond to demands for reform but arguably in a manner that would not threaten the overall status quo. This, perhaps, explains the Prime Minister's decision in April 2002 to appear twice a year before the Liaison Committee (see 2001-02, HC 984).

Promoting a parliamentary career

The introduction of additional salaries to select committee chairs was intended to create an alternative career structure to ministerial office. The Newton Commission recommended that the salary for a chair should be commensurate with that of a Minister of State (currently £38,000 in addition to the salary of an MP). The Norton Commission went further, suggesting that the chairs of certain major committees (such as the Treasury Committee and Public Accounts Committee) should receive the same salary as a Cabinet minister (currently £73,000 extra). The acceptance by the House of Commons of the Senior Salaries Review Commission's recommendation that the additional salary should be just £12,500 per annum (implemented from the start of the 2003-2004 parliamentary session) has done little to raise the status or profile of select committee work. Although reform-minded MPs remain positive and suggest that the additional salary could increase in future years, the current figure – described by some interviewees as 'derisory' – must be measured against the reality of executive influence within the House. During the 2001-2005 Parliament the executive consisted of 96 paid ministers and around 50 unpaid parliamentary private secretaries. This means that in the region of a quarter of all MPs hold a government post of some kind. The failure of Scottish and Welsh devolution to lead to a reduction in the size of the payroll vote, together with the Government's refusal to significantly reduce and limit the number of parliamentary private secretaries (as recommended by the Newton and Norton Commissions), arguably reflects the executive's reluctance to diminish the influence within the House of Commons provided by patronage.

Thus, the House of Commons still suffers from what King (1996) has described as a 'surfeit of partisanship' in which the vast majority of MPs perceive their first duty of loyalty is to party rather than Parliament. Backbenchers tend to view themselves, initially at least, as embryonic frontbenchers and political achievement is measured by ministerial rank rather than parliamentary achievement. Analysis of six major select committees between 1999-2000 and 2003-04 shows that turnover on some has actually increased in recent years, although the membership of the Defence and Health Committees has become more stable. Attendance on committees, meanwhile, has hardly improved and in some cases has declined (see Appendix 11). As yet, therefore, while the reforms to select committees have produced some benefits, notably in terms of encouraging more systematic scrutiny, the production of annual reports and the increased use of sub-committees to monitor arm's length bodies, there is little evidence that the basic culture of Westminster has been transformed. An alternative career structure has yet to be established.

The limitations of select committees exposed

The 2001-2002 parliamentary session marked the high point of parliamentary reform and modernisation. Important reforms had been agreed and approved on the floor of the House, such as additional payments for select committee chairs and an explicit statement of core tasks, though other reforms, notably the creation of a new Committee of Nomination designed to reduce the power of the whips, had not. From July 2002 the House of Commons entered a period of stability in which the reforms that had been agreed could be implemented and refined. This period of consolidation was reflected in the work of the Modernisation Committee. The July 2002 report *Modernisation of the House of Commons: A Reform Programme* (HC 1168) may have had a bold title but its contents were firmly located within the cautious, rather than the radical, camp. Its recommendations were aimed at improving the legislative process, making Parliament more accessible to the public and altering the Commons timetable and calendar.

The resignation of Robin Cook from the Government in March 2003 led to the appointment of John Reid as Leader of the House and a period of relative inactivity for the Modernisation Committee in which no reports were published. In June 2003 a Government reshuffle led to the appointment of Peter Hain as Leader of the House and a period of parliamentary politics that was notable for three reasons. Although, under Hain, the work of the Modernisation Committee concentrated more on the way that Parliament engages with the public (2003-04, HC 368) rather than fundamental questions about the balance of power between executive and legislature, a number of external factors thrust the issue of parliamentary reform back on to the political agenda towards the end of the 2001-2005 Parliament.

In March 2003 parliamentary pressure compelled the Prime Minister to break with precedent and provide the House of Commons with an opportunity to give its explicit support for the use of Britain's armed forces before they were sent into action in Iraq. Opening the debate, the

Prime Minister indicated that he was ready to resign if MPs voted against military action. The Commons rejected an anti-war motion by 396 votes to 217, a majority of 179, but the long-term importance of the vote, in parliamentary terms, was not the specific result but the fact that the vote had actually taken place. Intense parliamentary pressure had forced the Government to concede a vote in the House. This concession arguably undermined the prerogative that enables government to wage wars and sign treaties without parliamentary ratification.

The Liaison Committee, frustrated by the perceived lack of ambition by the Modernisation Committee, responded to events by vigorously criticising the executive and demanding reform. It acted as the arena through which the frustration of backbenchers could be expressed, particularly in relation to the limitations placed upon Parliament's access to 'persons, papers and records' compared to public inquiries. One area where this frustration manifested itself concerned the role of special advisers. The crucial point is not that special advisers exist but that their work is unaccountable to Parliament. Tension about the role of special advisers had been visible in the 1997-2001 Parliament (see 2000-01, HC 293) and increased during 2001-2005 as a number of select committees invited special advisers to appear before them but in each case had the request declined. In March 2002, for example, the Cabinet Office refused to allow Lord Birt, who was then acting as the Prime Minister's strategy adviser on transport issues, to give evidence as part of the Transport Committee's review of the Ten-Year Plan for Transport (see 2001-02, HC 655). Select committees had also unsuccessfully requested the attendance of advisers from the Performance and Innovation Unit in the Cabinet Office and the Prime Minister's Policy Unit.

Select committees not only faced problems in securing the attendance of special advisers but also ministers. In April 2002, for example, the Transport, Local Government and the Regions Committee formally reported to the House the refusal of Treasury ministers to give evidence to its Transport sub-committee as part of its inquiry into the public-private partnership for London Underground (see 2001-02, HC 771). The sub-committee had been informed during an evidence session that the Treasury had played, and continued to play, a central role in the design and planning of the whole scheme. The Committee recommended that the House of Commons make an order to a Treasury minister to attend.

Although the issue was discussed in the June 2002 Estimates Day debate, no opportunity was given to debate the proposed order. This was in clear contravention of the convention, first established in 1981, that time would be provided for a debate 'where there is evidence of widespread general concern in the House regarding an alleged ministerial refusal to divulge information to a select committee' (HC Deb 16/1/1981 c1312). In November 2003 the Science and Technology Committee encountered similar problems over securing the attendance of Home Office ministers as part of its inquiry into the scientific response to terrorism. In order to resolve the situation the Chair of the Science and Technology Committee was forced to agree with ministers formal constraints and limits on the scope of the inquiry which were seen as a clear limit on parliamentary accountability (see 2002-03, HC 415 paras.226-8; 2003-04, HC 169 para.34).

In July 2002 the first appearance by the Prime Minister before the Liaison Committee was used by several select committee chairs to challenge the Government on its continuing refusal to allow special advisers to appear before select committees (2001-02, HC 1095). Barry Sheerman, Chair of the Education and Skills Committee, and Gwyneth Dunwoody, Chair of the Transport Committee, both argued that the refusal by ministers to allow their special advisers to appear before select committees was inconsistent with the Government's vaunted commitment to reform the House. (It was also incompatible with the wider programme of constitutional reform aimed at increasing openness, transparency and accountability.) The Prime Minister responded by re-stating the convention that due to the formal classification of special advisers as temporary civil servants, it is up to ministers to decide who can best represent them before a parliamentary committee.

The difficulties faced by several select committees in securing witnesses and information from the executive were thrown into stark relief by the apparently open information regime enjoyed by several government-established public inquiries in 2003. The Hutton Inquiry into the death of Dr David Kelly (2004, HC 247), in particular, provoked parliamentary disquiet due to the striking contrast between the information released by the Government to that inquiry and the limited information made available to Parliament. The Hutton Inquiry had received original copies of internal documents, minutes of meetings, files and emails whereas select committees would only normally be provided with an official memorandum providing a précis of the information contained in the documents rather than the actual documents. The Inquiry also enjoyed full access to ministers, special advisers and senior civil servants from a range of departments.

The experience of the Foreign Affairs Committee provides a sharp contrast. When the Chair of that Committee wrote to the Prime Minister requesting his attendance; that of Alastair Campbell; the Cabinet Office Intelligence Co-ordinator; the Chair of the Joint Intelligence Committee; the Chief of Defence Intelligence; the Head of the Secret Intelligence Service; and the Director of GCHQ, none of them replied. After some time the Foreign Secretary informed the Foreign Affairs Committee that the Government had taken a decision that none of them would appear. The subsequent report by the Foreign Affairs Committee stated: 'We are strongly of the view that we are entitled to a greater degree of co-operation from the Government on access to witnesses and intelligence material' (2002-03, HC 813 para.6).

The experience of the Foreign Affairs Committee was not unique. During the 2001-2005 Parliament there were a number of instances when select committees requested specific documents and encountered a straight refusal (see Appendix 5). Moreover, parliamentary demands for specific documents were frequently declined on the basis that they were 'internal policy advice' and to release such information would adversely affect the candour of internal discussion. The Hutton Inquiry had, however, received a wealth of original documents which had then been published in their original form on the Inquiry's website. Select committee chairs, particularly those who had attempted to chair inquiries into topics which subsequently became the subject of a judicial inquiry, were exasperated by the clear contrast between the approach taken by the executive to providing information to public inquiries and that given to parliamentary inquiries.

The Government had also provided in private a far greater number and range of documents and witnesses to the Intelligence and Security Committee (ISC) while at the same time refusing to provide the same information to select committees. The ISC is not, however, a parliamentary committee. It is serviced by officials from the Cabinet Office, reports directly to the Prime Minister, and its nine members, although drawn from both Houses of Parliament, are appointed by the Prime Minister under the Intelligence Services Act 1994. The ISC meets in secret, publishes no transcripts and has no powers to compel the attendance of witnesses or to require the production of papers and records.

When established by the then Foreign Secretary, Lord Hurd, a commitment was given that the work of the ISC would not 'truncate in anyway the existing responsibilities of existing committees' (HC Deb 22/2/1994 c164). However, since the ISC was created successive Secretaries of State have, on several occasions, refused to allow the Foreign Affairs Committee (FAC) access to 'persons, papers and records' on the grounds that parliamentary scrutiny is carried out by the Intelligence and Security Committee (ISC) (for a review see 2000-01, HC 78). During both the 1997-2001 and 2001-2005 Parliaments the FAC repeatedly challenged this assertion and yet the executive has remained adamant that the FAC should not, indeed does not need, access to information regarding the work of the security agencies (c6123; c6062). The FAC has recommended that the ISC be reconstituted as a select committee of Parliament, thereby facilitating joint inquiries with the FAC, cultivating a more open way of working and providing the chair of the ISC with a seat on the Liaison Committee (2002-03, HC 813 paras.158-165; 2003-04, HC 440 paras.15-17). The Government rejected this recommendation, arguing that it saw 'no reason to change the current arrangements' (2003 c6062: 7).

At its meeting in October 2003 the Liaison Committee decided to review the workings of select committees with particular reference to the accountability of ministers and civil servants to Parliament. This topic was taken up during the next Liaison Committee session with the Prime Minister in February 2004 which began with a discussion of the implications of the Hutton Report for parliamentary scrutiny of the executive (2003-04, HC 310). Alan Williams, the Chair, requested that, in light of the clear disparity in relation to the information released to the Hutton Inquiry compared to the standard of information commonly made available to select committees, the Government should initiate a review of the rules relating to the availability of witnesses and information to select committees. The Prime Minister acceded to this request and on 6 July 2004 returned to the Liaison Committee and reported that the Leader of the House would be publishing a revised memorandum on the provision of information and witnesses before select committees in draft form towards the end of the 2003-2004 Session (2003-04, HC 310-ii Q144). However, Peter Hain's subsequent memorandum, in the opinion of many MPs, did not go far enough in amending the Osmotherly Rules and calls for greater access to 'persons, papers and records' continue to be made.

Parliamentary Questions

Complaints regarding the availability of information were not restricted to select committees. The standard of ministerial answers to Parliamentary Questions (PQs) and the number of 'blocked' answers also became a significant issue during the 2001-2005 Parliament. Towards the end of the previous Parliament the Government had sought to soothe the complaints of the PASC by publishing a revised Code of Guidance for officials preparing answers to PQs. However, in the next Session (2001-2002) the Government suffered an embarrassing setback when the Secretary of State for Health was forced to apologise to the Commons after an internal investigation revealed 'systematic falsification in recording the handling of parliamentary questions'. This included recording questions as having been answered when no such reply had been given to the Member or to the Official Report. The Secretary of State for Health, Alan Milburn, told the House:

> The Department of Health is fully committed to supporting the system of accountability to Parliament which underpins our democracy. We aim to provide timely and accurate responses to parliamentary questions. There has been a serious error in honouring this commitment, which I deeply regret (HC Deb 5/3/2002 c275W).

In its report of June 2002 the Procedure Committee accused ministers of consistently giving 'evasive and unhelpful' replies to oral questions (2001-02, HC 622 para.48). Although the Government vehemently rejected the accusation that ministers ever did anything other than 'take the answering of parliamentary questions extremely seriously' (2002 c5628 para.3) it did agree to support an integrated package of reforms made by the Procedure Committee.

Standing Orders were brought forward and subsequently approved by the House in October 2002 that attempted to increase the topicality of oral questions by reducing the deadline for tabling oral PQs from 10 days to three sitting days (five days notice for oral PQs to the Secretaries of State for Wales, Scotland and Northern Ireland). It was also agreed that MPs should be able to table oral PQs on any day after the last Question Time and before the minimum notice period, so as to allow those MPs who may be on constituency duties or select committee visits to put down their questions in advance. Ministers were empowered to make written ministerial statements, which no longer have to be in answer to a question, and such statements will be printed in the Official Record (this replaces so-called 'planted questions'). The timing of the shuffle (the process of drawing oral PQs to be put to ministers at question time) has also been brought forward from 6.30pm to 4.00pm in order to give MPs and ministers greater preparation time. Cross cutting questions would in future be put to ministers each week in Westminster Hall. Finally, the Procedure Committee's recommendation that the number of oral PQs per department in each daily slot should be reduced was also implemented.

The Procedure Committee had also complained that the current 'closed period' of nearly three months during the summer represented an unacceptable restriction on parliamentary scrutiny. In November 2001 the Government responded to this point and announced that it would in future answer PQs during a recess and these answers would be published in a special edition of the Official Report (HC Deb 15/11/2001 c871W).

While welcome improvements to the system these reforms do not represent the 'radical reform of both oral and written questions' in the way the Government described them (2004 c5628 para.7). The Procedure Committee had recommended a number of more significant reforms that were not supported by the Government. For example the Committee's June 2002 report had stated:

We also believe that the balance of power at Question Time between Minister and questioner is at present tilted too far in favour of the former, who can choose to give unhelpful or evasive replies, knowing that questioning will move on and he or she will shortly be 'off the hook'. We support the proposal by Lord Norton that the Speaker should give the Member who has asked a question the opportunity to ask a second supplementary after all supplementaries from other Members have been called. If this recommendation is implemented, the questioner will have the opportunity of some redress if the Minister has blatantly failed to address the original question (2001-02, HC 622 para.48).

The Government rejected this proposal on the basis that ministers would not seek to give 'evasive or unhelpful replies' (c5628 para.19) and that therefore this recommendation was simply unnecessary. The Procedure Committee has also suggested that provision for PMQs should be separately specified in Standing Orders so that any future changes would be open to debate and subject to the formal decision of the House. In essence, the Procedure Committee was demanding ownership of its own procedures as they related to PMQs. The Government also rejected this proposal on the basis that the Questions Rota has always been a matter for government and establishing it in a Standing Order may lead to inflexibility.

In July 2002 the PASC published its fifth report into PQs and parliamentary scrutiny, which covered the 1999-2000 Session (2001-02, HC 1086). The report noted concern regarding the executive's attitude to answering PQs and emphasised the reforms to the select committee system that were being advanced by the Liaison Committee and Modernisation Committee. While welcoming these reforms, the PASC stressed that, 'parliamentary questions are arguably the most important instrument of sustained accountability available to individual members, which is why they provide the focus for this committee' (2001-02, HC 1086 para.2). Statistics provided by the Table Office revealed that ministers refused to answer 3.39% of written questions to departments. This figure was remarkably constant with the figures of 3.23% in 1998-1999 and 3.39 for 1997-1998. However, once more the Committee criticised the fact that many departments were refusing to answer questions without providing any explanation (2001-02, HC 1086 para.16). Departments were also taking an increasing length of time to respond to the PASC's request to provide an explanation as to why certain questions had not been answered, which explained why the analysis of the 1999-2000 Session was not published until July 2002. The Committee also raised the issue of a continuing sense of dissatisfaction amongst a large number of backbenchers about the poor quality and inadequacy of ministerial replies. In criticising ministers the PASC drew upon the survey of MPs conducted by the Procedure Committee, as part of its inquiry into PQs in 2002 (2001-02, HC 622), which had found that more MPs were dissatisfied (28%) with the quality of answer received than satisfied (21%). This survey evidence complemented the increasing number of complaints received by the PASC.

Commercial confidentiality and parliamentary scrutiny

The increased use of the 'commercial confidentiality' exemption since 1997 was a particular concern for the PASC, particularly in light of the Government's commitment to public-private partnerships (PPPs) (see HM Treasury 2000). As the then Secretary of State for Health, Alan Milburn, emphasised in September 1999:

...partnerships between the public and private sector are a cornerstone of the Government's modernisation programme for Britain. They are central to our drive to modernise our key public services. Such partnerships are here and they are here to stay.

The Private Finance Initiative (PFI), under which private companies design, build and often manage public facilities (schools, hospitals, libraries, prisons, etc.) under a long-term contract, had been expanded since the election of the Labour Government in May 1997 – from nine projects with a total value of £667 million in 1995 to 65 projects with a total value of £7.6 billion in 2002 (HM Treasury 2003). A total of 563 PFI contracts reached closure by early April 2003, with a total capital value of £35.5 billion. Over £32.1 billion of the total has been signed since 1997 (see Flinders 2005). The 'commercial confidentiality' exemption refers to 'information whose unwarranted disclosure would harm the competitive position of a third party'.

The Government's commitment to PPPs had led to a rapid increase in the number of PQs to ministers being rejected on the grounds of 'commercial confidentiality' (see 2001-02, HC 1086 paras.21-24). As the Institute of Public Policy Research aptly observed in 2004, 'PPPs, like many forms of contracting for public services, disrupt traditional accountability structures'. The Government has consistently argued that the interests of private sector companies need to be protected, while MPs have sought to prioritise the public interest, particularly in light of the fact that there have been several high profile problems with PFI contracts. These include the contracts for the new computer system at the Passport Agency, the Benefits Payment Card Project at the Department of Social Security, the contract for the Royal Armouries in Leeds, the contract to build the Channel Tunnel Rail Link and the implementation of a new computer system within the Child Support Agency (see Ball, Heafy and King 2001; Broadbent, Gray and Jackson 2003; Pollack et al. 2001). The PASC recommended that the Government should in future ensure that the 'public interest is put above all other considerations' (2001-02, HC 1086 para.23).

The Government's response included the commitment to ensure that the relevant exemption is mentioned where ministers decline to answer PQs and to ensure that in future departments would reply within 20 days to the PASC request for an explanation as to why a specific question had not been answered (2002-03, HC 136). The PASC were, however, largely disappointed with the Government's specific reply, which failed to even mention the widespread concern regarding the 'commercial confidentiality' exemption, and the Government's approach to PQs more generally. The Committee raised the case of Steve Webb MP who had tabled a question to the Department for Work and Pensions only for it to be rejected by the minister on the basis that 'the information was not available' (HC Deb 18/3/2002 c155 W). Mr Webb then used the 1998 Data Protection Act to obtain internal records and discovered that the requested information had been available at the time the PQ had been tabled. The Committee also expressed concern at the increasing use of 'holding answers' by ministers. In its March 2004 report into PQs and ministerial accountability the PASC stated that 'the Government's approach has, at times, been characterised as minimising the opportunity for scrutiny of its actions' (2003-04, HC 355 para.2).

The impact of freedom of information

There is, however, little doubt that in recent years the presumption has changed significantly in favour of greater openness as a result of the introduction of the Code of Practice on Access to Government

Information in 1994 and subsequent legislation and official guidance. However, an anomaly exists in that any request for information from a member of the public to a government department or public body covered by the Code of Practice is automatically treated as a Code-application, irrespective of whether the request mentions the Code. The FOI Act, which became fully operational in January 2005, functions on the same basis. Where information is withheld the public body must tell the applicant why the information has not been released. If the applicant is not satisfied that the information has been justifiably withheld they can request an internal review and, if still dissatisfied, can take the case to the Information Commissioner.

This situation raises two issues. First, there is a divergence of accessibility between the public and MPs. In 2004 this led the PASC to investigate the degree to which MPs and peers were increasingly using the public route rather than the more opaque and cumbersome parliamentary channels. Secondly, annual monitoring reports published by the Department for Constitutional Affairs suggest that parliamentarians are increasingly using direct departmental requests for information rather than tabling PQs (see Appendix 6).

This increased use of direct requests to departments is largely due to a perception amongst some Members that PQs are not treated with sufficient priority by ministers and departments, and that parliamentarians are actually in a weaker position than members of the public when it comes to asking questions. Indeed, there is a requirement under the Code of Practice that applicants must be made aware of their right to appeal where a request for information is refused whereas in the House ministers are largely free to decide whether to answer a PQ which then prevents MPs from tabling questions on that topic for a length of time.

Moreover, as the PASC inquiries into PQs and ministerial responsibility have repeatedly demonstrated, the provision of information is highly dependent on the personal vagaries of individual ministers. Reshuffles and resignations often lead to the release of information that had previously been refused. From July 2002 MPs who received unsatisfactory answers to PQs have been able to refer them to the Chair of the PASC who will, where appropriate, take up the issue with the department concerned (2001-02, HC 1086 para.34). Although this procedure provides an extra dimension to parliamentary pressure and can on occasions result in more informative answers or an explanation as to why information is not being released, it does little to alter the basic fact that there is not much Parliament can do when faced with executive obstruction.

Parliamentary Questions and the nature of scrutiny

Although the actual number of occasions on which the Government has refused to answer a written PQ since 1997 is relatively small (Appendix 7) an analysis of those issues and topics where the Government has refused to answer PQs suggests two points. First, parliamentary scrutiny is dependent upon the quality, not quantity, of answers provided to questions. A common criticism of MPs is that replies to PQs tend to be designed to minimise the opportunity for careful scrutiny. Answers tend to be brief, curt and limited to a narrow interpretation of the information being requested. Indeed, an explanation for the high number of written PQs is that MPs will often have to table a series of questions, each time carefully refining the way in which the question is phrased and constructed, in order to receive a reply that provides even a glimpse of the information being sought. Lord Corbett, for example, described that when he was an MP it had often taken him 20 or more written PQs to get even a fraction of the information he sought (Flinders 2001: 95). The relatively low numbers of PQs that are rejected by ministers (as set out in Appendix 7) may therefore over-state executive co-operation as it does not include answers to PQs that are limited, incomplete or misleading.

This leads to a second point regarding the quantity versus quality dimension of parliamentary scrutiny. Although the Government has refused to answer only a comparatively small number of written PQs, arguably these questions relate to public interest matters and so parliamentary scrutiny is paramount. Thus the research of the PASC in the 2001-2005 Parliament demonstrated that ministers have repeatedly refused to answer questions on topics including GM crops, Railtrack, the Millennium Dome, expansion of Heathrow Airport, visa applications supported by ministers, the Hinduja brothers, special advisers, the future of the Post Office, the future of the BBC, and questions relating to the powers and responsibilities of a number of delegated or arm's length public bodies. There are clearly areas – such as national security and ministerial travel arrangements – where it has been generally accepted that answers to PQs concerning such topics should be refused. However, the majority of topics where the Labour Government has withheld answers do not fall within these areas, thereby fuelling speculation that answers are being withheld for political reasons rather than in the public interest. It is for this reason that the PASC has called for the introduction of an independent monitor who could investigate refusals to answer PQs to verify that the public, rather than political, interest had been paramount in the decision to withhold the requested information (2003-04, HC 355 para.13). The Government's position in relation to parliamentary scrutiny via PQs may seem anomalous given their decision to introduce a Freedom of Information Act, backed up with a right of appeal to a new Information Commissioner (and, if the applicant remains dissatisfied with the response they have received, to a new Information Tribunal). Indeed, there is concern within Parliament that the implementation of the FOI Act might leave Members disadvantaged in comparison to citizens, in obtaining information from government.

The Government has, however, firmly rejected the idea that Members would be disadvantaged as a result of the FOI Act (2003-04, HC 1262 para.2). If dissatisfied with an answer to a PQ, Members could pursue the normal parliamentary channels, tabling further questions, raising the issues on the Adjournment and complaining to the PASC. If a Member remained dissatisfied they could then write directly to the appropriate minister. This direct approach would be treated as a non-parliamentary request and would therefore be afforded all the provisions and appeal mechanisms afforded by the FOI Act. However, placing MPs in a weaker position than citizens, in terms of access to information, has the consequential effect of making Parliament appear even more peripheral to the concerns of the public. This should be viewed in the light of a resolution passed by both Houses in March 1997, which stated that:

> Ministers should be as open as possible with Parliament, refusing to provide information only when disclosure would not be in the public interest, which should be decided in accordance with the relevant statute and the Government's Code of Conduct on Access Government Information.

Explaining the Government's position in relation to PQs and freedom of information is not difficult. PQs, as a tool of parliamentary scrutiny, are deeply embroiled in the adversarial party political warfare of Westminster. As such ministers are well aware that the information released will not be examined in a mature and constructive manner but will inevitably be used, irrespective of the actual content, to attack the government. In 1996 Lord Howe outlined, with great candour, the true aims of PQs to the Public Service Select Committee: '...to secure damaging admissions, to secure damaging refusals, to secure damaging denials, to contrast the response of the minister with that which we wanted to offer, and so on, and very seldom were we actually after facts' (1996-97, HC 313-iii: 54). It is this entanglement of tools of parliamentary scrutiny within the broader party political mêlée that leads MPs to frequently describe PQs as a game – '...see if you can catch me out and I'll show you that you can't' as one MP has described it. The manner in which the political context limits the utility of PQs often surprises external observers. Lord Scott noted 'It surprised me when witnesses described PQs as a game – that is the antithesis of democratic accountability. On the other hand it would be naive not to see some realism in the point' (Flinders 2001: 74).

Scrutiny and ministerial accountability

Backbench frustration at the executive's perceived resistance to parliamentary scrutiny was further demonstrated by a highly critical report by the Foreign Affairs Committee published on 16 March 2004. The stark title of the report, *Implications for the House and its Committees of the Government's lack of co-operation with the Foreign Affairs Committee's Inquiry into the Decision to go to War with Iraq* (2003-04, HC 440), encapsulated the simmering tension between Parliament and Government. The report not only detailed the extent of the latter's refusal to co-operate but also demonstrated that, although select committees are entitled to take an issue to the floor of the House, they are still heavily reliant on the goodwill and co-operation of the executive. The Foreign Affairs Committee noted, 'When we began our inquiry in June 2003, we were hopeful that we would receive full co-operation from the Government...this was not forthcoming (para.2).'

The only way in which the committee could have sought to insist on the attendance of official witnesses or the production of official papers would have been to make a Special Report to the House, or to table an appropriate motion. Either course of action would have required the Government's agreement for a debate to be held in government time (para 4). The Foreign Affairs Committee (FAC) openly admitted that the Commons' powers in relation to forcing the executive to co-operate with the mechanisms of parliamentary scrutiny are, in practice, unenforceable due to tight party whipping and large majorities (2003-04, HC 440 para.13). In order to publicise the issue and place pressure on the Government the FAC invited the House to consider and reach a view on the following questions:

- What procedures should apply when a relevant minister refuses to appear before a Committee of this House?

- What procedures should apply when a minister refuses to allow a named civil servant or other official within his area of responsibility to appear before a Committee of this House?

- What procedures should apply when a minister refuses to supply papers or records to a Committee of this House?

The questions became particularly pertinent in October 2004 when the Leader of the House published the Government's revised *Code of Practice on Departmental Evidence and Response to Select Committees* (see 2003-04, HC 1180). The revision clearly reflected a cautious rather than a radical approach to reform and is best seen as adjusting rather than rebalancing the power relationship. The Government's reluctance to bring forward proposals that may weaken its control on the provision of information to the House is clearly evident in two key areas. First, the revised guidance remains wedded to the primacy of the convention of ministerial responsibility, which in practice allows ministers to control the information on which they will be held to account. Indeed, the memorandum is saturated with the assertion that 'civil servants who give evidence to a Select Committee do so on behalf of their Ministers and under their directions'. In evidence to the Liaison Committee the Leader of the House repeatedly emphasised that the convention of ministerial responsibility remains 'the bedrock of the relationship between the executive and the Commons'. Secondly, the draft document suggests that the paragon of the Liberal view of the constitution, in which Parliament can act independently of the executive, still exists as reality long after most observers have dispelled it as constitutional fiction (see Flinders 2002). For example, the draft guidance notes (para.29) that, where a select committee finds itself in dispute with a minister over the provision of information and where there is widespread general concern in the House, the government would seek to provide time for the House to express its view. However, as both the Liaison Committee and Foreign Affairs Committee emphasised during the 2001-2005 Parliament, potential recourse to the floor of the Commons is something of a feeble sanction due to tight party management via the Whips Office.

It is for these reasons that, while welcoming the explicit presumption within the revised Code that information and identified witnesses would be provided, particularly in relation to special advisers, the Liaison Committee was less than impressed by the new guidance. Indeed, the Chair opened the evidence session with the Leader of the House by stating that the proposed changes were 'most striking for their modesty' (2003-04, HC 1180 Q2). The revised Code, as set out in the Leader of the House's memorandum, offered more continuity than change – a fact not overlooked by members of the Liaison Committee. The Chair of the Environmental Audit Committee, Peter Ainsworth, challenged the Leader of the House that the revised memorandum included no new formal powers or unequivocal rights for select committees: 'The thing that worries me is that this great new presumption in favour of disclosure does not seem to change anything.' The memorandum had been modernised to some extent but essentially the revisions did nothing to alter the fact that select committees would remain reliant on the goodwill of the executive.

The revised guidance illustrates the enduring centrality of individual ministerial responsibility within the British Constitution or, more accurately, how this convention is interpreted and employed by the executive. The importance of the convention of ministerial responsibility is arguably not so much that it provides a sword of accountability – a mechanism through which Parliament can scrutinise and hold the executive to account – but that it acts as an accountability shield, through which the executive can legitimate the restriction of 'persons, papers and records' to the House (Flinders 2000). The executive maintains that, as it is ministers and not their officials who are constitutionally responsible to Parliament, it can only be for ministers to decide upon the individuals and documents through which that accountability can be secured. To do otherwise, so the Leader of the House argued, would risk undermining the candour with which officials could advise ministers and risk undermining the impartiality and anonymity traditionally ascribed to civil servants.

While this view has some validity it veils the reality of modern governance in which successive governments have implemented public management reforms that have been based on the delegation of responsibility to named officials who have a far higher public and media profile because of the position they hold. Indeed, the demand by select committees to have a more direct and open relationship with the heads of executive agencies and executive non-departmental public bodies, without the shadow of ministerial instructions limiting the provision of information, is based upon the experience of ministers engaging in 'blame games' (Hood 2002).

Under the current constitutional arrangements ministers can shift responsibility for specific incidents or issues onto an agency chief executive by interpreting the cause of the problem as 'operational'. Information that might contradict that interpretation, particularly if it suggests the failing was due to an inappropriate ministerial policy decision, can be withheld from Parliament through the control of information and limits placed upon witnesses. Moreover, the candour argument is not a conclusive barrier to more openness in the policy-making process. Indeed, other Westminster style jurisdictions, such as New Zealand and Australia, have introduced reforms that have achieved more transparency while maintaining an environment in which senior officials can engage in frank and full discussions with ministers. These debates and arguments are by no means new. During the 1980s and 1990s arguments based upon the need to uphold and protect the convention of ministerial responsibility were similarly used by Conservative Governments to reject parliamentary reform proposals (see 1996-97, HC 313). However, it is conspicuous that a Labour Government that was explicitly committed to shifting the balance of power between the executive and Parliament when in opposition should also be relying on such dated logic after two full terms of office.

Scrutiny and the Lords

Since the 1999 House of Lords Act removed the vast majority of hereditary peers, the second chamber has displayed a new and increasingly combative confidence vis-à-vis the executive (see Appendix 8). In 2000, Lord Alexander, Chair of the House of Lords Delegated Powers and Deregulation Committee, reflected upon the executive control in the House of Commons and the increasing number of defeats that the Government had suffered in the Lords, and asked: 'can the Lords be the new guardians of our democracy?' Since then, the Lords has refused to defer to executive pressure and pushed at the limits of the convention that it must consider the government's business without unreasonable delay. For example, in March 2004 the Lords voted at the end of its Second Reading to send the Constitutional Reform Bill (Lords) to a select committee for further scrutiny and deliberation – only the second time a Bill had been treated in this way since 1917. The Lords also became increasingly active in relation to the scrutiny of Statutory Instruments. For example, in February 2000 the Lords annulled the Greater London Authority Rules 2000 (the first time the Lords had ever rejected a negative instrument) and defeated the Greater London Authority (Election Expenses) Order (only the second time the House had ever rejected an affirmative instrument). The Lords also resurrected a method of challenging and holding the government to account unknown for nearly a century when it amended the motion on the Queen's Speech in December 2003 – the first time since 1914. There has also been an expansion in the amount of committee work done by the Lords. Select committees on the European Union, Delegated Powers and Regulatory Reform, and the Constitution, have produced a constant flow of influential publications that reflect not only a less adversarial environment but also the fact that members are appointed according to their professional expertise and specialist knowledge. Despite this progress in the Lords, the Modernisation Committee has failed to make a connection between its strategy for Commons reform and the wider debate about the role and relationship with the second chamber.

Parliamentary Scrutiny: Conclusion and Implications

In general, modernisation-as-efficiency has had more success than modernisation-as-scrutiny, Tony Wright MP (2004: 870).

Parliament matters. Britain remains a parliamentary state and narratives that describe the 'eclipse of Parliament' risk fundamentally misunderstanding the location of power within the British constitutional framework (Lenman 1992). In 2001 Hazell wrote, 'It is a puzzle why a government so committed to modernisation and reform has been so feeble when it comes to the House of Commons'. There is no puzzle. Despite a wealth of largely prosaic literature lamenting its demise, Parliament remains the central locus of legitimate state power in Britain. An executive that did not control the Commons would be in office but not in power. That power resides in Parliament explains consecutive governments' solicitous management of majorities within the House and their reluctance to countenance reforms that may dilute their position.

It is, however, important to appreciate that in the vast majority of select committee inquiries and parliamentary questions, the current Labour Government has provided a full and satisfactory account and disputes regarding the provision of witnesses and information are the exception rather than the rule. Even where the Government has been reluctant to release information and witnesses, such disputes have generally been resolved through informal discussion and compromise. Relations between department officials and select committees are in the main constructive and harmonious. This largely amicable relationship is based on the fact that ministers are fully aware of the power of Parliament to make or break careers. Ministerial reflections, like for example those of Lord Hurd (1997) and William Waldegrave (1995), illustrate that parliamentary appearances are given paramount attention. Ministers must treat Parliament with respect because they need to retain the support of their parliamentary party. An unprepared minister would appear incompetent and lacking in ability. It is also necessary for ministers to appear to take Parliament seriously to uphold the notion that Parliament really is enforcing parliamentary accountability. By paying lip service to ministerial responsibility, which serves them so well, ministers undermine calls for new methods of accountability or parliamentary reform. Officials also understand that being caught unprepared in front of a select committee may damage their minister and, therefore, their own career. This fact underpins the assertion that Parliament matters. However, it is because Parliament matters so much that a perverse logic exists that encourages ministers to muzzle or limit its scrutiny capacity.

It is for this reason that parliamentary scrutiny exerts a constant influence on the decision-making structure within British governance due to the potential that any decision may at some point in the future be subject to a parliamentary question or committee inquiry. Parliamentary scrutiny therefore fulfils an *ex ante* function that arguably ensures the wishes of Parliament are taken into account or expected standards of behaviour are upheld by ministers and officials in order to avoid later embarrassing scrutiny in the House. Parliamentary scrutiny is also not confined to formal channels. The role and importance of informal scrutiny channels, such as ministerial meetings with MPs, the parliamentary party or one of the numerous all-party subject groups, are often put forward as reasons not to overstate the apparent weakness of formal parliamentary scrutiny mechanisms, such as select committees. Indeed, MPs have in the past suggested that the shortcomings associated with the formal mechanisms of parliamentary accountability are somewhat appeased by the existence of informal and/or party mechanisms of accountability (see Flinders 2001). The value of these informal scrutiny channels is limited, however, by the fact that they rely heavily on the good will of ministers and they take place in private with no public record provided. But a frequent complaint of backbenchers is that the procedural and timetable changes to the Commons have actually undermined the potency of these informal scrutiny channels due to the fact that there are fewer opportunities for backbenchers to 'collar' ministers in the Lobby or corridors of the Palace of Westminster.

However, it would be wrong to assume that backbenchers are impotent in the face of executive intransigence. The 'Norton view' (1983), that parliamentary control of the executive can be achieved through attitudinal change on the part of MPs has been increasingly evident during the 2001-2005 Parliament. The reforms to the select committee system and the Prime Minister's decision to appear twice-yearly before the Liaison Committee were to some extent the result of backbench pressure and frustration with the lack of parliamentary reform. However, on balance it appears the executive has generally controlled the pace and extent of even these reforms through tight party management of its majority within the House. There is also a clear correlation between the political saliency of an issue and the executive's willingness to co-operate. The majority of parliamentary questions and inquiries revolve around issues that are not highly salient in that they focus on detailed aspects of administration or broad policy areas. However, where the focus of parliamentary scrutiny falls upon an issue of serious public concern or where ministers are directly involved (and could therefore be criticised) the executive is clearly less wiling to co-operate, although it is arguably exactly in this latter category of issues that parliamentary scrutiny is most needed.

Nonetheless, several important reforms to the system have been agreed and implemented during 2001-2005 which have increased Parliament's capacity to scrutinise the executive. As Wright (2004: 871) has stressed, parliamentary reform 'is a matter of exploiting cracks and getting wedges in doors'. The level of parliamentary frustration and debate about the need to shift the balance of power between the executive and Parliament towards the end of the 1997-2001 Parliament created an opening into which a number of small but potentially significant wedges could be placed. These include paying select committee chairs an additional salary, adopting guidelines for core tasks for select committees, establishing a Scrutiny Unit to support the committee structure and the appearance of the Prime Minister twice a year before the Liaison Committee. The wedges may well provide the basis for further strengthening and extension. In time the gradual accumulation of these wedges may begin incrementally to alter the balance of power.

There are signs that Parliament is already trying to take advantage of these wedges and press for further changes. In June 2002 the Procedure Committee (2001-02, HC 622 para.60) recommended that the questioning of the Prime Minister in committee be extended with more frequent appearances, perhaps every six to eight weeks. Although the Government politely rejected this recommendation (2002 c5628 para.24) it illustrates that Parliament's appetite for scrutiny powers has been whetted but not yet satisfied. The parliamentary vote in March 2003 on the Iraq war not only set a precedent from which future governments will find it very difficult to depart, as the Chancellor of the Exchequer, Gordon Brown, recognised in May 2005, but also offers encouragement that, at some point, a wider parliamentary incursion into the executive's range of prerogative powers will be mounted. Moreover, wedges set in one sphere of parliamentary activity may well act as the catalyst for fissures in others. This theme will be developed in the concluding chapter; the next section examines modernisation in relation to the style, form and working arrangements of Parliament.

(iii) Modernising the style, form and working arrangements of Parliament

The previous two sections concentrated on changes to the legislative process and measures impacting on Parliament's ability to scrutinise the executive and hold it to account. However, improving the law-making process and strengthening Parliament vis-à-vis the government were not the only objectives of Labour's modernisation programme. As the Commons Leader underlined in a parliamentary debate on modernisation, just three weeks after Labour's 1997 election victory, improving MPs' working arrangements and updating the style and form of parliamentary proceedings also constituted an important part of the agenda. This section examines the chronology of change in relation to the style, form and working arrangements of Parliament, looking in particular at reform of sitting hours, the parliamentary calendar and parliamentary papers. In addition, it considers the attempts made to update Parliament's media facilities, to widen public access to the building and to improve the management and security of the House. In so doing, it highlights the core fault line that frequently serves to divide opponents and proponents of modernisation; namely, the different perceptions that each hold about the proper role of an MP and the primacy of the Commons Chamber within Parliament.

Initial cosmetic changes

'There is a feeling', Ann Taylor told MPs early on in the course of the Labour Government, 'that, while it is good to reinforce our parliamentary traditions, we might be able to modify some aspects of them without any loss of ceremony or dignity' (HC Deb 13/11/1997 c1064). Among the first examples of such modifications were the changes to division procedures, alterations to the style, form and content of the Order Paper, and a complete overhaul of the explanatory material for Bills. Taylor later reported to the House that the enthusiastic response which greeted the new Order Paper 'was much more significant than I had thought it would be – Members seemed really to welcome the change. Members of the press in particular were somewhat puzzled by the fact that they could now understand what was going to happen later in the day' *(Ibid)*. While noting that such changes were 'not exactly earth shattering', Taylor argued that they nonetheless 'mark real progress and there is certainly much more to do. Some people said a few months ago, "When will you modernise Parliament?", as if modernisation were one event. None of us on the Committee thought of modernisation as one event. It is a process and we have started well on it, but there is much more work to come' (*Ibid* c1065).

There was more, but not under Taylor's direction. A year into the new Government she was moved from her position as Commons Leader and appointed Chief Whip. Although the move was widely seen as a promotion, some believed that Taylor had lost momentum following the rejection of her plans to introduce a form of electronic voting to the Commons. The failure of that proposal owed to the conservatism of backbenchers on both sides of the House – a characteristic that Margaret Beckett, Taylor's successor as Leader of the House, was also said to share. As noted earlier, Beckett is now widely regarded as an executive-minded Commons Leader who had little interest in advancing the modernisation agenda. Yet she oversaw a number of significant changes to Parliament that were warmly welcomed by modernisers, most particularly the establishment of Westminster Hall – a parallel debating chamber which was opened in 1999 to provide an additional forum for MPs to initiate debates and discuss select committee reports. As well as offering more parliamentary time, supporters of the innovation hoped that the semi-circular Westminster Hall – located in the Grand Committee Room and modelled on a parallel chamber employed by the House of Representatives in Australia – would facilitate a less adversarial style of politics than that frequently practiced in the Commons Chamber.

Initially approved by the Commons on an experimental basis, the use of Westminster Hall was extended following a report by the Modernisation Committee (1999-2000, HC 906), which concluded that the experiment had been a success. The report noted that, in addition to giving MPs more opportunity to raise issues and quiz ministers, it had increased television coverage of parliamentary matters, notably on regional news and current affairs programmes. However, the report emphasised that it was just as important to acknowledge what Westminster Hall had not done. Specifically, it had not acted as a vessel through which the Government could expedite its legislative programme; the business in Westminster Hall was 'other' business which would otherwise not have taken place. The report thus concluded that the chamber had proved 'an exciting and major new development which should give the lie to those who claim that the House of Commons is hopelessly antiquated and impervious to any change whatever'.

Westminster Hall has since become a permanent fixture and won plaudits from many backbench MPs for increasing their ability to secure adjournment debates and raise local and national issues with the relevant ministers. Indeed, in each of the three sessions between 1999 and 2002, Westminster Hall 'provided an additional 24, 27 and 31 percent of the total time available in the House…In an average year it is likely that there will be 320 such debates, about 130 of the longer 90 minute slots and 190 of the half-hour debates' (Rogers & Walter 2004: 270). Aside from the increased scope to gain a parliamentary airing, many Members were pleased with the less adversarial atmosphere of the new chamber. Joan Ruddock told the House that 'the seating arrangements have made an immense difference to the way in which debates take place. We do not have the confrontational behaviour and attitudes in Westminster Hall that we see and hear in the Chamber. I suggest that there is much more deliberation of greater depth by Members who wish to air an issue which may be party political, but not in the partisan manner that is adopted in this Chamber' (HC Deb 20/11/2000 c43). Similar sentiments were expressed by Paul Tyler and Sir George Young, illustrating the Hall's cross-party appeal. But despite general approval, a minority of MPs were, and remain, outspoken critics of the new chamber. Eric Forth, a constant thorn in the side of modernisers, derided the new chamber as 'little more than a facility for electronic press releases', while Gwyneth Dunwoody raised the spectre of executive dominance, alleging that Westminster Hall is 'a cynical reform to keep people out of the way' (*Ibid* c52). For these parliamentarians, the new chamber has proved little more than a talking shop in which backbenchers can sound off without really posing any real threat or problem to the Government.

Such critics were also opposed to the introduction of deferred divisions, another measure implemented during Margaret Beckett's tenure as Commons Leader. This measure allows votes on certain categories of parliamentary business to take place, not immediately after the moment of interruption, but on the following Wednesday afternoon by MPs marking a ballot paper. Explaining the rationale behind the proposal, Beckett told the House (HC Deb 7/11/2000 c222) that:

> Members are aware that the process of voting itself has been used to detain hon. Members late at night, even when no debate was possible, or when only a handful of hon. Members were engaged. I know that many colleagues, on both sides of the House, feel that the sheer unpredictability of being so detained, without even being sure that there will be a vote at all, is one of the worst aspects of our procedures – [Interruption.] I am aware that not everyone shares that view, but it is a view that is legitimately held. We are all perfectly well aware that 999 times out of 1000, those matters are so handled not as a matter of principle, but as a matter of tactics.

Deferred divisions were thus presented as a modification that would bring more certainty to parliamentary business and allow MPs to use their time more productively. But sceptical observers countered that the change would contribute to earlier finishing times, thereby reducing the amount of time MPs spent holding the government to account in the Chamber. Furthermore, it was alleged that deferred divisions would make it easier for whips to manage the troops by divorcing debate from decision, effectively turning MPs into automatons (Rogers & Walters 2004: 373). As with Westminster Hall, opponents felt that the change to voting procedure was camouflaged as a 'modernising' measure in order to hide the fact that it was, in reality, a calculated manoeuvre initiated by the executive with the aim of making it easier to control backbenchers and secure government business.

Sitting arrangements and the parliamentary calendar

The central gripe of self-styled 'traditionalists' is that modernisation is more about improving efficiency and convenience than strengthening Parliament vis-à-vis the executive. Hence, critics were particularly antagonised by the alteration of Parliament's sitting hours (see Appendix 10 for details of changes to sitting arrangements since 1997). This issue has since become perhaps the most controversial aspect of the modernisation process, yet it was initially dismissed by Ann Taylor as peripheral to 'Labour's true project for Parliament'. Indeed, Taylor was explicitly opposed to any significant change in sitting arrangements designed to make Parliament more representative of standard business practice, asserting that 'a simple-minded call for a nine-to-five day and a five-day week is a chilling prospect for me as an MP for a Northern constituency, let alone as the mother of two children' (1996). In her view, the problem of late night sittings, which had become frequent in the 1970s and 1980s, had effectively been solved by the Jopling Reforms. Moreover, she argued that those reforms had provided a better balance between MPs' parliamentary and constituency work by freeing up 10 Fridays in each session. There was, therefore, no need for further change.

Although the Jopling Reforms undoubtedly had a positive effect in terms of reducing the amount of late night sittings, many MPs disagreed with Taylor that further reform was unnecessary. Indeed, according to some, the greatly increased number of women MPs elected in the new Parliament meant that the issue became more, not less, salient after 1997 (Seaton & Winetrobe 1999). But it was not until Taylor was succeeded by Margaret Beckett as Leader of the House that the Modernisation Committee formally addressed the issue. In late 1998, the Committee published a set of proposals for changes to the parliamentary calendar which recommended that the House should begin at 11.30am on Thursdays, with the 'moment of interruption' coming at 7.00pm instead of 10.00pm (1998-99, HC 60). The change was presented by Beckett as designed to reduce pressure points during the session and to make parliamentary arrangements 'more family friendly' (*The Independent* 1 July 1998). The Commons subsequently accepted the report's recommendations, which were implemented for an experimental period that was later extended to the 1999/2000 session. Although the new Thursday sitting hours proved generally popular, some within the Commons expressed disquiet at the change and, perhaps more significantly, at the source of the proposal. Sir Nicholas Winterton, himself a member of the Modernisation Committee, asked (HC Deb 16/11/1998 c1000-01) fellow MPs:

Is not one of the problems facing the House the fact that this is a House of Commons matter, yet we are considering Government proposals? With no disrespect to the Leader of the House, for whom I have great admiration, I am not sure that I believe that the [Modernisation] Committee should be chaired by a member of the Government and Cabinet. That is the problem. We are debating Government proposals which the Government want to get through when it should be entirely a House of Commons matter; proposals should be put forward by the House of Commons through the Modernisation Committee.

A minority of MPs simply opposed the change itself; in particular the justification that it sought to create a 'family friendly' House. Sir George Young warned that any such explanation could backfire, highlighting the negative press coverage that the change attracted, stating that 'far from the reforms helping to elevate the status of the House, the way in which the Government presented them made that task even harder' (*Ibid* c1000).

Others argued that reform had not gone far enough and asserted that, even allowing for the new arrangements, Parliament could still scarcely be described as 'family friendly'. They pointed to the fact that 87 sittings of the House during the 1998/99 had continued after 10.00pm, rising to 99 in the following session. Pressure for further reform of sitting hours was thus maintained and eventually bore fruit with the publication of the Modernisation Committee's report recommending timetabling of legislation, which imposed stricter time limits on debates and ensured that most sittings of the House would finish at 10.00pm on Mondays to Wednesdays. Explaining the reason for the change, a Government source told *The Guardian*: 'Most people have come to the conclusion that you cannot allow legislation to be taken through the House at 3.00am', before adding 'This is the biggest shake-up at Westminster since the introduction of select committees in 1979' (6 July 2000).

Cook creates a stir

In fact, the new sitting arrangements instituted under Margaret Beckett were minor compared to the much more radical changes instigated by Robin Cook, following his appointment as Commons Leader in June 2001. As noted previously, Cook approached the job with a more comprehensive view of parliamentary modernisation than either of his predecessors, and the new sitting arrangements that he piloted were part of a broader package of reforms designed both to improve the efficiency of Parliament and strengthen the ability of MPs to hold the executive to account. Cook believed that the most pressing case for modernisation was 'not the balance between Parliament and government but the growing gulf between Parliament and the public'; a situation that he felt was not helped by the Commons' loving preservation of 'the image and the working methods of a bygone age'. Cook felt that such methods had to be updated if Parliament was to regain authority and restore public confidence in its work (2003: 23).

Changes to its working hours thus formed an important part of Cook's vision of a modern House of Commons. His proposals, which were narrowly agreed by the House in October 2002, involved: keeping the original hours for Monday at 2.30pm to 10.00pm; bringing the sitting time on Tuesdays and Wednesdays forward to an 11.30am start, with the moment of interruption coming at 7.00pm; and retaining the 11.30am start on Thursdays, but bringing the moment of interruption back to 6.00pm. In addition, the reform package also included changes to the parliamentary calendar (publishing it for the year ahead for the first time) and the introduction of a two-week sitting period in September, to punctuate the traditional long summer recess.

As well as being an attempt to improve Parliament's image by aligning its hours of work more closely with those kept by society generally, the new timetable was also designed to improve Parliament's ability to set the news agenda. As Cook told the House (HC Deb 29/10/2002 c700):

Under current arrangements, exchanges in Parliament on major policy take place in the afternoon. We are all professional communicators; no one in the Chamber would plan a press conference for 4pm. If we are serious about the elected Parliament of the people setting the agenda for public debate, we need to start earlier in the day so that questions, statements and opening speeches are made in the middle of the day rather than when many of our constituents approach the end of their working day...announcements should be made to Parliament at a time when the lunchtime bulletins can report what has been said rather than speculating about what might be said.

Despite this appeal to self-publicity (which can exert a powerful pull on many MPs) the Commons debate on the motion dealing with the new hours revealed opinion to be heavily divided. Whilst some Members argued in favour of the new hours – with many pointing to the importance of making Parliament's working arrangements more 'family-friendly' and representative of normal business practice – others argued that the changes would make no difference to public perceptions of Parliament and would actually be a retrograde step, compressing the parliamentary day and putting more pressure on MPs. Moreover, many Members – particularly those representing constituencies outside the South East – claimed that the new timetable would be injurious to the overall culture of Parliament by curtailing the vibrant social life evident in the Commons most evenings. The diversity of opinion over hours of work was reflected in the narrowness of the votes to change them, with approval being given to the motion relating to Tuesdays by 274 votes to 267 and an amendment to drop the provisions for Wednesdays defeated by 288 votes to 265.

The new sitting arrangements were instituted for a fixed period – until the end of the Parliament – at which point they would be reviewed and subjected to another vote in the House. Although supporters hoped that this period would enable the House to acclimatise to the new hours, critics remained steadfast in their opposition. With views so polarised, it was little surprise that when the House voted on the sitting arrangements in January 2005, the result was a classic Westminster fudge: MPs chose to keep the earlier start time on Wednesdays, reduce an hour on Thursdays but return to the 2.30pm start on Tuesdays. Consequently, over five sitting days the House of Commons now has four different start times. Although the compromise reached over sitting hours would seem to suit no-one, it would appear that the issue has now been resolved – at least for the foreseeable future.

Enhancing engagement

Cook's partially successful attempt to modify sitting arrangements was partly aimed at making Parliament appear more representative of, and understandable to, the world beyond Westminster. That objective arose from concerns which had been building since the mid-1990s, about the apparently increasing problem of public disengagement from politics. That trend was identified in various surveys which recorded falling public confidence in the political process against the backdrop of sustained low levels of turnout in parliamentary and other elections after 1997. As a result, various bodies within Westminster began to investigate ways of helping Parliament to better communicate its work to the public.

In 2000, the House of Commons Commission, which supervises House administration, adopted as one of its core aims: 'to improve public understanding and knowledge of the work of the House and to increase its accessibility'. That same year, under Margaret Beckett, the Modernisation Committee published a report setting out several proposals aimed at improving facilities for the media within Parliament. On the basis of that report, four recommendations were subsequently approved by the Speaker and put into effect. These lifted the ban on the use of tape recorders, by journalists, in the Gallery of the House; permitted the use of tape recorders by journalists in sittings in Westminster Hall; permitted filming in Members' own offices; and allowed still photographs of visiting dignitaries. However, partly because television, radio and press media are largely beyond Parliament's control, the Committee also investigated ways that new technologies could be utilised to enable it to bypass the intermediaries and broadcast its activities directly to the public. Webcasting of parliamentary proceedings over the internet is perhaps the most notable example of this and was introduced in 2002 on an experimental basis, having been given explicit backing by Robin Cook in his memorandum of December 2001 (2001-02, HC 440). The idea was also pushed by the Broadcasting Committee (2002-03, HC 786) and became a permanent feature in 2003.

After becoming Leader of the House in June 2003, Peter Hain made the engagement agenda a key focus of the Modernisation Committee's work, holding an inquiry in 2004 into how Parliament could build a more direct and interactive relationship with the public. The report of that inquiry, *Connecting Parliament with the Public* (2003-04, HC 368), published in June 2004, made a series of recommendations including proposals for the construction of a Visitor Centre, a parliamentary newsletter, and the provision of Educational 'Parliament in Action' Tours for members of the public to supplement the existing tourist-targeted historical guides. The most contentious recommendation, however, was the Committee's proposal to remove from Standing Orders the term 'Strangers', which had traditionally been used to refer to members of the public present within the parliamentary estate. For Hain, the phrase sent 'a dreadful signal to every citizen and every voter' and was detrimental to Parliament's image in the eyes of the public. The proposal to remove it was debated and agreed by the House in late October 2004. Since then the House of Commons Commission has formally responded to the

Committee's report (2004-05, HC 69), indicating that progress is already being made in several other areas outlined in *Connecting Parliament with the Public*, notably in relation to the production of clearer public information about the work of Parliament.

Although *Connecting Parliament with the Public* was a largely uncontroversial inquiry, it nevertheless managed to divide parliamentarians. For some, such as Eric Forth, the inquiry was 'ridiculous' and did not even touch the fundamental questions about political disengagement. For others, notably Hain, it was about 'mak[ing] this place feel more modern in every respect so that it actually resembles the kind of buildings and institutions that people normally go into rather than something that is a hangover from medieval times'. Hain believed the investigation served to highlight Parliament's institutional conservatism, which he claimed could block even the most modest reform proposals. The Labour Member, Joan Ruddock, similarly described Parliament as the 'worst organised place' she had ever worked in: 'At the institutional level it requires complete root and branch change, particularly in its management. At every level it stays in the past.' The pressure for root and branch reform of the management structures within Westminster has grown in the aftermath of several security breaches in recent years. One such breach, in which pro-hunt protestors invaded the Commons Chamber while the House was sitting, prompted Hain to declare that Parliament was 'log jammed by vested interests and fiefdoms…There is an emerging consensus not only for radical reform to Parliament's security but also for the whole way this place is run…We need professional management…we must enter the 21st century' (*The Times*, 18 September 2004). Although it is only five years since the Braithwaite Report looked into the management systems of the House, a further inquiry now seems likely.

Modernisation of style, form and working arrangements: explaining disagreement

Many of the changes outlined above, viewed in isolation, could scarcely be described as revolutionary or epoch-making. Yet almost every one generated controversy and disagreement. For many MPs, measures such as earlier sitting times, the creation of Westminster Hall and improved public access were regarded as sensible steps towards making Parliament a more dynamic, efficient and welcoming place. Others, however, labelled them a deliberate attempt to destroy the effectiveness of the House of Commons. Eric Forth perhaps exemplifies those who take that position to its extreme, arguing that the principal duty of an MP is to be in Westminster, holding the Government to account and participating in debates and votes: 'I regard that as the main part of my duties...If [a] Member of Parliament chooses to spend less and less time here and more and more time talking to people in the constituency, the thing has got hopelessly out of balance' (HC Deb 20 /11/2000 c52).

However, successive surveys, and indeed attendance in the House, suggest that most MPs do not share that vision. A survey of the 1997 intake carried out by *House Magazine* showed that 86% judged 'being a good constituency member' to be the most important role of an MP. More recently, a poll found that a third of MPs felt dealing with constituents' grievances was either the most, or second most, important part of their job (Hansard Society 2001: 142-143). Helen Jackson possibly articulated the outlook of the majority when she told the Commons that (HC Deb 20 /11/2000 c48):

The job of Member of Parliament has many aspects which need to be balanced, and certainly involves more than working in the House...The relationship between what we learn and hear about our constituents' hopes and fears and the way we make those hopes and fears our concern when we are in the House scrutinising, debating and voting on legislation is the substance of democracy. To argue that one of them is somehow subservient to the other misses the whole point of our role.

Thus, the campaign for better office accommodation, modern facilities and extra staff was fought most determinedly by those who would be described as 'modernisers'. This group is probably becoming predominant in Parliament, as a more demanding public encourages MPs to expand their extra-parliamentary role, facilitated by new information and communication technologies such as email and the internet, which enables the physical relocation of staff to constituency offices (Gay 2005b). Furthermore, the provision of live television coverage of Parliament in MPs private offices discourages attendance in the Commons. Consequently, many lament the effect that new offices and resources have had on the general culture of Westminster. As one respondent told our inquiry, 'When MPs didn't have offices there was more action – more politics – in the committee corridors and cafes. The chamber is emptier now.' In truth, new offices and information technologies have brought many benefits and are here to stay. But the effect of such modernisation has arguably helped to draw the gaze of MPs away from the chamber. Moreover, the pressure to focus on local issues and constituency cases at the expense of scrutiny and legislative work is likely to be sustained. In such circumstances, unless steps are taken to combine scrutiny and accountability with constituency duties, Parliament will be further weakened and the executive subjected to even fewer checks.

4 | Conclusions and recommendations

Parliamentary modernisation since 1997 has been punctuated by great hope and positive advances on one hand, and deep frustration and backward steps on the other. The period began with great expectations for positive change, stimulated by the election of a Labour Government committed to modernising Parliament in order to make the institution stronger, more efficient and more appealing to the outside world. However, although a number of significant reforms have been enacted over the last eight years, particularly during the 2001-2005 Parliament, the objectives outlined by the Labour Government have not been fully met. Despite some improvements, Parliament remains in many ways an inefficient and, some would allege, largely ineffective institution. Likewise, it continues to suffer from low public esteem. Moreover, while there have been some important changes in the relationship between the executive and Parliament, it remains clear that the balance of power remains firmly in the lap of the former. In terms of an overall assessment of the period since 1997, therefore, this report concurs with the view of Tony Wright that: 'In general, modernisation-as-efficiency has had more success than modernisation-as-scrutiny'.

The reason for this outcome stems in part from flaws in the prime mechanism designed to create a modern Parliament. The Modernisation Committee, formed soon after Labour's 1997 election victory, failed to produce a blueprint for what it wanted a modern scrutinising Parliament to look like. With no clear end point for reform, the work of the Committee was shaped by the interests and outlooks of its personnel, especially its chair and key members and officials. Between 1998 and 2001, Margaret Beckett, the longest serving Chair of the Committee – and Leader of the House – displayed little or no interest in strengthening Parliament. Consequently, apart from a number of important changes to the legislative process during Ann Taylor's brief spell as Commons Leader in 1997, the Modernisation Committee concerned itself during the Blair Government's first term with largely superficial matters and steered well clear of issues concerning the accountability of the executive.

Going into the 2001 general election, therefore, there was widespread dissatisfaction both inside and outside Westminster about the nature and extent of parliamentary modernisation, certainly as far as shifting the balance of power was concerned. However, a confluence of factors that year opened a 'window of opportunity' that Robin Cook, a new and more parliamentary-minded Leader of the House, was able to exploit. In the wake of a recent general election, buoyed by a groundswell of political demand for change, and armed with a reform agenda formed from the recommendations of several commissions and committees that had reported around that time, Cook piloted a raft of important measures through Parliament designed to deliver modernisation-as-efficiency in tandem with modernisation-as-scrutiny. Key developments included the introduction of additional payments to select committee chairs, reforms to select committees and Parliamentary Questions, and the twice-yearly appearance of the Prime Minister before the Liaison Committee. The last of those developments emerged outside the formal modernisation process, but nonetheless owed something to the momentum and pressure for change that had built up.

The impact of these reforms is not yet fully known, but although their long-term effect may be to strengthen Parliament in ways that the Government did not anticipate when they were passed, as things stand it would be inaccurate to claim that the balance of power has shifted decisively away from the executive. That said, it would be equally mistaken to argue that no change of any significance has been affected. Cracks have been exposed into which, as Tony Wright has said, wedges may be pushed. In other words, while the modernisation measures enacted over the past eight years may not have achieved the objectives outlined at the start of the process, at least some opportunities have emerged that can be built upon and extended. In this concluding section, we make a number of recommendations as to where existing fissures should be exploited and new openings created.

Parliament matters. Those who claim that it has become an irrelevance are mistaken. The Palace of Westminster remains at the apex of British democracy, but its pre-eminent position is under threat. Parliament is dominated by the executive, undermined by low levels of public confidence and declining interest in its affairs, and challenged by the growth of alternative sources of power: the European Union, the judiciary, quasi-autonomous public bodies, the media, global financial markets, regulators and so on. To restore confidence in its role and revitalise its work Parliament needs to reassert and re-establish its own identity. Primarily, it needs to take more control of running its own affairs.

As a first step, **the House of Commons should establish a Business Committee responsible for managing the parliamentary timetable**. At present the informal 'usual channels' benefits the executive over the interests of backbenchers and the opposition. A Business Committee would bring a greater certainty to the parliamentary timetable and involve the main political parties in the management of business. Another key role of the Business Committee would be to ensure that the Commons determined its own Standing Orders and protected the Commons' interests against any encroachment by the executive. The idea of a steering committee to organise business is not new and has been widely recommended by other reviews of Parliament (Hansard Society 1992, 2001; *Strengthening Parliament* 2000; *Parliament's Last Chance* 2003; Rogers & Walters 2004). Government backing has never been forthcoming, largely because the executive fears a Business Committee would lead to a serious loss of control over parliamentary business. But if, as numerous ministers have declared down the years, more accountable government leads to better government, then this must surely be a positive step. Moreover, it is significant that many other Parliaments have a bureau or steering committee which decides and manages parliamentary business. For example, the model has recently been incorporated into the Scottish Parliament under the title 'Bureau' – chaired by the Presiding Office and including representatives from parties with five or more MSPs, weighted to party share – and illustrates a very different form of business organisation and also provides a forum for discussion and negotiation on matters of parliamentary administration and concern.

Secondly, **we recommend that the Modernisation Committee should be restructured in order to give more weight to the views of Parliament**. As previously described, the nature of its composition – with the Leader of the House, a Cabinet Minister – in its chair, meant that the Committee was at times easily diverted from an agenda concerned to increase accountability towards one more in tune with the executive's thirst for greater efficiency. For some, the presence of a member of the executive at the heart of the Modernisation Committee is a fatal flaw that can only be solved by its dissolution. However, while the Committee has undoubtedly been a double-edged sword, its abolition would be a backward step. As one participant told our inquiry,

> There is a fallacy that if the Modernisation Committee didn't exist with a cabinet minister in the chair, somewhere there would be another committee getting on with sensible reform; who was going to be doing it?...The Procedure Committee [which considers the practice and procedure of the House, and the conduct of public business] can make recommendations until the cows come home but the government can just ignore them all.

But if the Modernisation Committee is to continue to exist, perhaps there is a way that Parliament's voice could be amplified within it. **The appointment of the Chair of the Procedure Committee, who already sits on the Modernisation Committee, as its permanent Deputy Chair would provide an influential, expert parliamentary voice and give the Committee's leadership a degree of constancy that is currently disturbed with each change of Commons Leader.** Furthermore, there should be an assumption that the Procedure Committee Chair should always be a member of the opposition party, as is the case with the Chair of the Public Accounts Committee and the Standards and Privileges Committee.

Alongside the Modernisation Committee, the Liaison Committee has emerged since 1997 as a champion of Parliament, publishing a number of influential reports that threw down a gauntlet to the Government and helped build momentum for demands to strengthen the legislature vis-à-vis the executive. To further enhance its position, **the Liaison Committee should be restructured and reduced in size**. As one contributor to this inquiry noted, the Liaison Committee's rejection of proposals to slim it down and differentiate between scrutiny and domestic committees means that 'we have a bizarre situation in which the chair of the catering committee has a hand in questioning the Prime Minister every six months'. **By removing the chairs of domestic committees from its membership, the Liaison Committee would** become less unwieldy and more able to provide direction and co-ordination of parliamentary activity.

There are three areas where a reformed Liaison Committee could give immediate parliamentary leadership. First, as noted earlier, the information provided to the Hutton and Butler inquiries has thrown into stark relief the limited range of information generally provided to select committees. The House of Commons, through the Liaison Committee, should not submissively accept the minor changes to the Osmotherly Rules that were offered by the Leader of the House in October 2004. The rules regarding the appearance of officials before select committees have always been 'Whitehall rules' and Parliament should not feel bound by them nor afraid to draw up its own Code of Conduct. **The House of Commons should consider taking ownership of the current rules regarding the provision of 'persons, papers and records' to select committees by asking the Liaison Committee to devise a set of guidelines that could be passed on the floor of the House in a manner akin to that followed for the core tasks for select committees.** More generally, Parliament needs to ensure that its Members get fair treatment under the Freedom of Information Act. At a minimum the resolution of March 1997, which linked ministerial answers to PQs with the Code of Access to Official Information, should be replaced with an updated version that includes the presumption that the provisions of the Freedom of Information Act should now form the benchmark for ministerial answers.

Second, the Liaison Committee should display parliamentary leadership and vigour by supporting the PASC's recommendations of February 2005 relating to public inquiries (2004-2005, HC 51). There has been a long-term diminution in Parliament's role in the process of inquiries throughout the 20th century. The draft *Inquiries Bill*, which was introduced for consideration into the Lords in November 2004, would further restrict the role of Parliament while creating new powers for ministers to impose indefinite restriction notices or orders on public access to the proceedings and evidence of an inquiry. It would also make the obligation of public access subordinate to this power of restriction – a direct reversal of the presumption in favour of openness to be found within the 1921 Tribunals of Inquiry (Evidence) Act – as well as giving ministers new powers to terminate an inquiry where it is viewed as investigating beyond its original remit. Public inquiries represent a critical mechanism of public accountability and executive scrutiny which can complement and deepen parliamentary oversight. But they are an accountability tool that is controlled by the executive rather than Parliament; it is ministers who decide whether to establish an inquiry and, if so, what its remit and powers will be and how and when the final report will be published. **As the PASC notes, 'Parliament now has to decide whether it wants to reclaim territory it has lost as far as inquiries of this kind are concerned'. A valuable bulwark against executive dominance would be the rejuvenation of parliamentary commissions of inquiry, reporting to the House as whole or a specific select committee, rather than to ministers.** The PASC has suggested that Standing Order No.145 should be amended to enable the Liaison Committee to consider the value of a proposal that a specific matter of public concern involving ministers should be the subject of a formal inquiry and, if so, to report a resolution to the House of Commons for its consideration. Although in practice these parliamentary commissions of inquiry would be used infrequently, a formalised procedure for their establishment would represent another minor shift in the balance of power from the executive to Parliament.

The third key area in which the **Liaison Committee should take the lead relates to a formal review and evaluation of the select committee reforms that have been implemented since 1997. This should take place towards the middle of the next Parliament and would involve the Liaison Committee reviewing the efficacy of recent reforms and assessing the need for further change.** This review would examine core tasks, resources, payment for select committee chairs, and the Scrutiny Unit. What seems already apparent is that the select committee system needs to better reflect the evolving structure of the British state. Currently, select committees are largely based around the traditional departmental structure and yet the greater part of British governance takes place beyond ministerial departments in the form of public-private partnerships, non-departmental public bodies and other forms of delegated governance. **A select committee or joint committee of both Houses dedicated to the scrutiny of this delegated sphere of governance would complement the work of the departmentally related select committees while also illuminating the innate complexity of modern governance.**

Furthermore, any review should consider changes to the structure of select committees, particularly the case for increasing the number of members who sit on them. (The Hansard Society's Scrutiny Commission proposed that there should be an assumption that all backbench MPs should sit on at least one select committee). **Consideration should also be given to piloting the formation of one or two committees that would combine the functions of select and standing committees.** Such combined committees are the norm in most other Parliaments, including in Scotland and most of Western Europe. A piloted approach, with full evaluation, would allow a judgement to be made as to whether such a combined system would enhance Parliament's scrutiny and accountability functions.

The establishment by the Lords, in 2003, of the Merits of Statutory Instruments Committee to serve as a sifting mechanism to identify those Statutory Instruments that are important and merit further debate or consideration, serves as a model that the Commons should follow. It also represents a challenge to the Commons which risks ceding crucial functions to the Lords. The Commons, in the form of the Procedure Committee, has already made a strong case for such a Committee, in 1996 and 2000 (HC 152; HC 48). It is the Government that needs to be persuaded. The Government's argument that a Merits Committee would place greatly increased demands on parliamentary time seems unconvincing in the face of such widespread and severe criticism of the current methods of scrutinising delegated legislation. **We urge the Government to reconsider and establish a Merits Committee in the Commons to enhance the scrutiny of this vital area of legislation.**

In addition to the creation of a House of Commons Merits Committee, two further, sensible procedural changes would improve Parliament's operation and increase its scrutiny powers. First, **there should be a presumption that all legislation will be produced in draft form to allow for increased scrutiny.** Encouragingly, the Government has already voiced its intentions to move in this direction and to build upon the positive steps that have been made. Secondly, and relatedly, **greater use should be made of Special Standing Committees**, which would allow committees to hear outside expert opinion on a Bill and potentially enable members to work in a more collegiate fashion. Although the powers to use such special committees already exist, they are little used because their formation requires the agreement of ministers who fear their use will delay the passage of legislation and weaken party control. This attitude is short-sighted, given the obvious inadequacies of the present system of standing committees, in which the majority of MPs, as Peter Riddell notes, ignore their scrutinising duties and simply get on with constituency correspondence or – depending on the season – their Christmas cards: 'The result is a mass of hastily considered and badly drafted Bills, which often later have to be revised' (2000: 12).

The shortcomings of standing committees encapsulate in microcosm the reason for low public interest and confidence in Parliament. The misleading view that Parliament is tangential to modern politics is to some extent perpetuated by textbooks that fail to discuss recent reforms and continue to misrepresent Members as lobby fodder (see, for an example, Ward 2004). However Parliament does not help itself. Debate in the House of Commons, according to one well-known media commentator, appears to those outside as some kind of 'parallel universe' with its 'farmyard noises which signify approval or scorn' making the 'business of democracy seem cheap' (Paxman 2002: 98). A critical task for Parliament is, therefore, not just to achieve significant change to its capacity to hold the government to account but also to ensure that such change enables the public to engage more closely and meaningfully in its work.

One obvious method would be to **make petitions a more significant feature of the work of Parliament**. At present they are governed by strict rules about wording and there is little sense that petitions to Parliament result in any concrete action on the part of MPs. Many are submitted to Parliament each year but they rarely, if ever, translate into action. This is in contrast to the Scottish Parliament where the Public Petitions Committee plays a pivotal role in connecting the public and the legislature. All petitions go to the Committee which then assesses the merits of each submission by consulting with the executive, MSPs and, if necessary, taking evidence from individuals and organisations. The Committee filters out petitions where action is already being taken or where the case is weak. Where there is a case to be answered the Committee refers petitions on for further consideration. **We recommend that a Petitions Committee should be established in the House of Commons to assess issues of public concern and, if appropriate, to make referrals for debate or committee inquiry**.

The opportunity and need for immediate action

Parliament and the executive enjoy a fluid and dynamic relationship. Much of the tension and friction involved in this relationship is played out and resolved through informal channels. It is often difficult for those not actively working within the Palace of Westminster to detect, recognise and understand the role and importance of these unofficial channels of communication. The system is much more complex and complicated than it looks from the outside. Therefore, to describe Parliament as an irrelevance or to talk of its eclipse (Lenman 1992) is to misunderstand the depth and complexity of parliamentary politics. Nor is such a position supported by empirical research. One of the central revelations of Stothard's 2003 shadowing of the Prime Minister, for example, was not how little Parliament mattered but conversely how much time and energy the Prime Minister and other members of the Cabinet spent meeting backbenchers and various all-party parliamentary groups. Stothard's *30 Days* represents a rejoinder to much of the academic literature which perpetuates the myth of parliamentary impotence.

Parliament quite clearly does have some control over the executive but whether it has sufficient control is another matter. This study of parliamentary modernisation since 1997 reveals a situation in which the House of Commons is still largely reliant on the good-will of the executive to provide the information on which it can be held to account. On the relatively small number of occasions when the executive refuses to co-operate with a select committee inquiry or declines to answer a PQ (or answers in a limited or misleading manner) the current balance of power effectively insulates the executive from parliamentary censure. There are, however, a number of reasons to be optimistic.

The issue of parliamentary reform and the relationship between Parliament and the executive is becoming an issue of increasing debate and controversy. There is a sense that the current situation is unsustainable and must at some point be addressed. The Liaison Committee, *Parliament First* group of Members, the All Party Parliamentary Reform Group, and the Cross-Party Group on Reform of the Second Chamber are advancing this agenda. The executive is well aware of heightening backbench pressure for reform and has acknowledged that it is willing to support (or at least not block) reform proposals that have cross-party support. One of Peter Hain's last duties as Leader of the House involved considering how best to revise the Codes of Conduct relating to the provision of information to Parliament. In advancing reform Parliament now has a number of 'wedges and cracks' through which it can seek to open up and further develop its scrutiny of legislation and the administration of the British State. This may involve increasing the additional payments for select committee chairs or further developing the role and personnel of the Scrutiny Unit.

As Evans (2003) has emphasised constitutional reforms tend to have 'spillover' and 'spillback' effects in that reform in one area is likely to lead to demands for similar reforms or procedures to be implemented elsewhere. The creation of a Scottish Parliament and a Welsh Assembly and reforms within the European Parliament, for example, have seen the introduction of innovative new procedures and frameworks for scrutinising the wider state sector and an active role for scrutiny committees in senior public appointments (see Denton and Flinders 2005; Flinders 2004b). The creation of a Petitions Committee and a Business Committee in the Scottish Parliament have led to increasing discussion regarding the possibility of creating similar bodies in London. In time, it is likely that cross-fertilisation will lead to demands for similar procedures to be adopted at Westminster. Similarly, the fact that elections to the Scottish Parliament, Welsh Assembly and London Assembly have been established using a proportional system (modified Additional Member System) and fixed-term elections makes the continued use of a plurality system for Westminster increasingly difficult to justify. Indeed, the Labour Government's ambivalence towards even opening up a debate about altering the voting system for Westminster is possibly the clearest illustration of its commitment to maintaining a strongly majoritarian model of democracy in Britain.

There are also clear areas of 'unfinished business' where the current constitutional configuration is arguably indefensible – reform of the second chamber being the most pressing example. A reformed second chamber designed to complement and support the work of the Commons may go some way towards shifting the balance of power between the executive and Parliament as a whole.

It is critical that Parliament acts now to address the weaknesses outlined in this report. The low turnout (61%) at the May 2005 general election once again underlines the fact that a significant proportion of the population have become disconnected from the formal political process. What many hoped was a blip in 2001 has turned into a sustained problem, with worrying implications. As one former Leader of the House commented, 'Parliament's authority rests on public confidence'. If it is to restore such confidence it must take advantage of the current momentum for reform and build on the opportunities created in recent years not just to shift the balance of power between Parliament and the executive but to close the growing gulf between Parliament and the public. This report has highlighted a possible future course for parliamentary modernisation. It is up to parliamentarians to follow it.

Appendix 1: List of Interviews

Interviewee	Date of Interview	Interviewer
Anne Campbell	15 September 2004	Declan McHugh
Robin Cook	10 November 2004	Declan McHugh
Gwyneth Dunwoody	7 September 2004	Matthew Flinders
Mark Fisher	7 July 2004	Alex Brazier
Eric Forth	21 June 2004	Alex Brazier
Peter Hain	8 September 2004	Declan McHugh
Oliver Heald	7 September 2004	Matthew Flinders
Baroness Jay	13 September 2004	Declan McHugh
Lord Norton of Louth	22 June 2004	Declan McHugh
Peter Riddell	6 September 2004	Matthew Flinders
Joan Ruddock	16 September	Alex Brazier
Meg Russell	16 November 2004	Declan McHugh
Lord Robert Sheldon	14 September 2004	Declan McHugh
Paul Tyler	6 September 2004	Matthew Flinders
Sir Nicholas Winterton	9 September 2004.	Alex Brazier
Tony Wright	29 June 2004	Declan McHugh
Sir George Young	8 September 2004	Matthew Flinders

Appendix 2: Modernisation Committee Reports 1997-2005

Session 1997-1998	Title
First Report	*The Legislative Process*
Second Report	*Explanatory Material for Bills*
Third Report	*Carry-over of Public Bills*
Fourth Report	*Conduct in the Chamber*
Fifth Report	*Consultation Paper on Voting Methods*
Sixth Report	*Voting Methods*
Seventh Report	*The Scrutiny of European Business*
Session 1998-1999	
First Report	*The Parliamentary Calendar: Initial Proposals*
Second Report	*Sittings of the House in Westminster Hall*
Third Report	*Thursday Sittings*
First Special Report	*Work of the Committee: Second Progress Report*
Session 1999-2000	
First Report	*Facilities for the Media*
Second Report	*Programming of Legislation and Timing of Votes*
Third Report	*Thursday Sittings*
Fourth Report	*Sittings in Westminster Hall*
Session 2000-2001	
First Report	*Programming of Legislation*
Session 2001-2002	
First Report	*Select Committees*
Second Report	*Modernisation of the House of Commons: A Reform Programme*
Session 2002-2003	
First Report	*Modernisation of the House of Commons: Programming of Bills*
Session 2003-2004	
First Report	*Connecting Parliament with the Public*
Session 2004-2005	
First Report	*Sitting Hours*
Second Report	*Scrutiny of European Business*

HC Ref./Date of Publication
HC 190 29 July 1997
HC 389 9 December 1997
HC 543 9 March 1998
HC 600 9 March 1998
HC 699 29 April 1998
HC 779 5 June 1998
HC 791 17 June 1998
HC 60 7 December 1998
HC 194 13 April 1999
HC 719 19 July 1999
HC 865 1 November 1999
HC 408 10 April 2000
HC 589 6 July 2000
HC 954 6 November 2000
HC 906 13 November 2000
HC 382 2 April 2001
HC 224 12 February 2002
HC 1168 5 September 2002
HC 1222 3 November 2003
HC 368 16 June 2004
HC 88 11 January 2005
HC 465 22 March 2005

Appendix 3: Leaders of the House 1997-2005

Leader of the House	Dates
Ann Taylor	May 1997 – July 1998
Margaret Beckett	July 1998 – June 2001
Robin Cook	June 2001 – March 2003
John Reid	March 2003 – June 2003
Peter Hain	June 2003 – May 2005
Geoff Hoon	May 2005 –

Appendix 4: Core Tasks for Select Committees, adopted by the Commons, May 2002

Objective A: To examine and comment on the policy of the department.	
Task 1	To examine policy proposals from the UK government and European Commission in Green Papers, White Papers, draft guidance etc., and to inquire further where the Committee considers it appropriate.
Task 2	To identify and examine areas of emerging policy, or where existing policy is deficient, make proposals.
Task 3	To conduct scrutiny of any published draft Bill within the committee's responsibilities.
Task 4	To examine specific output from the department expressed in documents or other decisions.
Objective B: To examine the expenditure of the department.	
Task 5	To examine the expenditure plans and out-turn of the department, its agencies and principal NDPBs.
Objective C: To examine the administration of the department.	
Task 6	To examine the department's Public Service Agreements, the associated targets and the statistical measurement employed, and report if appropriate.
Task 7	To monitor the work of the department's Executive agencies, NDPBs, regulators and other associated public bodies.
Task 8	To scrutinise major appointments made by the department.
Task 9	To examine the implementation of legislation and major policy initiatives.
Objective D: To assist the House in debate and decision	
Task 10	To produce reports which are suitable for debate in the House, including Westminster Hall, or debating committees.

Appendix 5: Government Refusal to Release Documents to Select Committees 2001-2005

- The Defence Committee asked for copies of 'Lessons learnt' reports from Commanding Operations in Operation Telic which were prepared as part of the MOD's overall assessment of the operation. This request was refused. The Chairman expressed his displeasure at the refusal in the course of an evidence session in September 2003. The Ministry of Defence subsequently reiterated its refusal.

- The Environmental Audit Committee has complained about the refusal of departments to publish their sustainable development reports. The Treasury claimed that these were an internal part of the spending review process.

- The Foreign Affairs Committee had difficulty in procuring actual Foreign and Commonwealth Office telegrams (i.e. official correspondence) in its Sierra Leone inquiry and more recently was refused access to official papers relating to the Bali bombing, on the grounds that these were being supplied to the Intelligence and Security Committee.

- The International Development Committee eventually resorted to an appeal to the Ombudsman under the Code of Access of Official Information to seek copies of ministerial correspondence between the Foreign and Commonwealth Office and the Department for Trade and Industry on the Ilisu Dam.

- The Quadripartite Committee (Defence, International Development and Trade and Industry Committees, and Foreign Affairs Committees) encountered a refusal to provide – even in confidence – an analysis of the costs and benefits to Tanzania of acquiring a military air traffic control system, with the Foreign and Commonwealth Office claiming that to do so would risk either breaching commercial confidences or harming the frankness and candour of internal discussion.

Source: *Liaison Committee Scrutiny of Government: Select Committees after Hutton*, Note by the Clerks published as a memorandum of the Committee, 8 January 2004.

Appendix 6: Analysis of Applications for Information under the Code of Practice on Access to Official Information 1998-2002.

Year	1998	1999	2000	2001	2002
Individuals	15.1%	30.6%	26.5%	33.1%	40.0%
Businesses	49.2%	17.2%	17.3%	14.4%	8.0%
MPs/Peers	1.9%	1.4%	10.1%	18.4%	24.0%
Media	1.5%	4.8%	1.3%	3.6%	16.0%
Academics	4.5%	4.8%	3.0%	2.0%	5.0%
Charities/Lobbies	2.9%	1.6%	1.9%	10.7%	4.0%
Others	24.9%	39.6%	39.8%	17.8%	3.0%
Total no. of requests	7459	3424	5351	4111	3614

Note: The Department for Constitutional Affairs' monitoring procedures only monitor requests for information where the Code of Practice is specifically mentioned, information for which a fee is paid or are refused under a Code exemption.

Source: HC 355 (2003-2004) para.6

Appendix 7: Written Parliamentary Questions (WPQs) and Ministerial 'Blocking'

Session	Total WPQs	WPQs Blocked	Source
1996-1997	18,439*	140 (0.75%)	HC 820 (1997-1998)
1997-1998	29,120*	324 (1.11%)	HC 821 (1998-1999)
1998-1999	32,139	311 (0.96%)	HC 61 (2000-2001)
1999-2000	35,931	380 (1.05%)	HC 1086 (2001-2002)
2000-2001	16, 642	146 (0.88%)	HC 355 (2003-2004)
2001-2002	67, 283	807 (1.20%)	HC 355 (2003-2004)
2002-2003	50, 859	908 (1.79%)	HC 449 (2004-2005)
2003-2004	49, 814	819 (1.64%)	HC 449 (2004-2005)

Note. The memorandum annually provided to the Public Administration Select Committee (since 1996) does not include those answers refused due to 'disproportionate costs' nor does it provide a complete digest of answers that could be interpreted as blocking further questions, or an absolute statement of what may not be asked.

Statistics on the number of WPQs declined by departments due to the 'disproportionate costs', involved in collecting the requested information are not centrally collected but are likely to far exceed the proportion interpreted as 'blocked' by the Table Office. For example, in the 1998-1999 Session while 311 WPQs were 'blocked' a further 732 were not answered for reasons of 'disproportionate costs'.

* Figures provided by the House of Commons Table Office.

Appendix 8: Government Defeats in the House of Lords 1992-2004

Session	Government Defeats
1992-93	19
1993-94	16
1994-95	7
1995-96	10
1996-97	10
1997-98	39
1998-99	31
1999-2000	36
2000-2001	2
2001-2002	56
2002-2003	88
2003-2004	64
2004-2005	37

Appendix 9: Key Reports and Government Replies

Date	Title	Ref./Session
March 2000	**Liaison Committee** *Shifting the Balance: Select Committees and the Executive*	HC 300/1999-2000
May 2000	**Liaison Committee** *The Government's Response to the First Report from the Liaison Committee on Shifting the Balance: Select Committees and the Executive*	Cm. 4737 2000
July 2000	**Liaison Committee** *Independence or Control? The Government's Reply to the Committee's First Report of Session 1999-2000 – Shifting the Balance: Select Committees and the Executive,*	HC 748/1999-2000
March 2001	**Liaison Committee** *Shifting the Balance – Unfinished Business,*	HC 321/2000-2001
Dec. 2001	**Modernisation Committee** *Modernisation of the House of Commons: A Reform Programme for Consultation, Memorandum submitted by the Leader of the House*	HC 440/2001-2002
Feb. 2002	**Modernisation Committee** *Select Committees*	HC 224/2001-2002
March 2002	**Liaison Committee** *Select Committees: Modernisation Proposals*	HC 692/2001-2002
Sept. 2002	**Modernisation Committee** *Modernisation of the House of Commons: A Reform Programme*	HC 1168/2001-2002

Appendix 10: Major changes to House Sitting Arrangements since 1998

	December 1998	January 2003	January 2005*
Monday	2.30pm-10.00pm	2.30-10.00pm	2.30pm-10.00pm
Tuesday	2.30pm-10.00pm	11.30am-7.00pm	2.30pm-10.00pm
Wednesday	2.30pm-10.00pm	11.30am-7.00pm	11.30am-7.00pm
Thursday	11.00am-7.00pm	11.30am-6.00pm	10.30am-6.00pm
Friday	9.30am-2.30pm	9.30am-2.30pm	9.30am-2.30pm

* These hours came into effect in May 2005.

Appendix 11: Use of Sub-Committees and Turnover of Membership in Six Selected Cases

	1999-2000		2000-01	
No of sub committees*	5		5	
Committee	**Attendance (%)**	**Turnover (%)**	**Attendance (%)**	**Turnover (%)**
Culture Media and Sport	80.7	0	75.8	0
Defence	80.1	36	62.7	0
Health	69.5	36	60.8	0
Home Affairs	75.6	9	59.1	0
International Development	65.8	9	69.1	0
Treasury	72.3	25	65.1	8

Numbers apply to total number of sub-committees established by Commons Select Committees

2001-2		2002-3		2003-4	
12		17		19	
Attendance (%)	Turnover (%)	Attendance (%)	Turnover (%)	Attendance (%)	Turnover (%)
83.5	0	73.6	0	73.6	18.2
83.04	9	74.58	36.4	72.9	9.1
84.4	0	73.7	27.3	74.3	9.1
76.7	0	71.1	63.6	71.8	18.2
75.5	36.4	64.4	18.2	59.6	18.2
72.9	0	74.1	27.3	72.7	18.2

Appendix 12: Parliamentary Scrutiny Reforms
2001-2005

- The deadline for tabling oral parliamentary questions was reduced from 10 days to three

- Answers to PQs now provided when Parliament is in recess

- Written statements replaced 'planted' questions

- Select committees adopted a framework of core tasks

- Scrutiny Unit established to support select committees

- Select committees empowered to establish sub-committees and joint-inquiries with other committees on their own initiative

- Committees empowered to exchange papers with the Scottish Parliament and Welsh Assembly

- Additional payments introduced for select committee chairmen

- Prime Minister to appear before the Liaison Committee twice a year

- Parliamentary vote on the war in Iraq

- Ministers take questions on cross-cutting issues each week in Westminster Hall

Bibliography

Allen, G. (2001) *The Last Prime Minister: Being Honest about the UK Presidency* (London: Graham Allen).

Amery, L. S. (1947) *Thoughts on the Constitution* (London).

Ball, R., Heafy, M. & King, D. (2001) 'The Private Finance Initiative: A Good Deal for the Public Purse or a Drain on Future Generations', *Policy & Politics*, 29:1, 95-108.

Beetham, D., Byrne, I., Ngan, P., & Weir, S. (2003) 'Democratic Audit: Towards a Broader View of Democratic Achievement', *Parliamentary Affairs*, 56:2, 334-347.

Brazier, A. (2000) *Systematic Scrutiny, Reforming the Select Committees*, (London: Hansard Society).

Brazier, A. (2000) *Parliament and the Public Purse: Improving Financial Scrutiny*, (London: Hansard Society).

Brazier, A. (2003) *Parliament at the Apex: Parliamentary Scrutiny and Regulatory Bodies*, (London: Hansard Society).

Brazier, A. (ed.) (2004) *Parliament, Politics and Law Making: Issues and Developments in the Legislative Process* (London: Hansard Society).

Broadbent, J., Gray, A., & Jackson, P. (2003) 'Public-Private Partnerships', *Public Money and Management*, 23:3, 135-136.

Conservative Party (2002) *Delivering a Stronger Parliament*, (London: Conservative Party).

Cook, R. (2001) Speech to the Hansard Society, London, 12 July 2001.

Cook, R. (2001b) 'A Modern Parliament in a Modern Democracy', State of the Union Annual Lecture, Constitution Unit, University College London, December 2001.

Cook, R. (2003) *The Point of Departure* (London: Simon & Schuster).

Cook, R. & Maclennan, R., (2005) *Looking Back, Looking Forward. The Cook-Maclennan Agreement, Eight Years On* (London: New Politics Network).

Cowley P. & Stuart M. (2001) 'Parliament: Mostly Continuity, But More Change Than You'd Think' in Ridley F. & Rush M. (eds.) *UK 2001: Into the Second Term*.

Cowley, P. & Stuart, M. (2001) 'Parliament: A Few Headaches and a Dose of Modernisation', *Parliamentary Affairs*, 54:2, 235-257.

Cowley, P. & Stuart, M. (2003) 'Parliament: More Revolts, More Reform', *Parliamentary Affairs*, 56:2, 188-204.

Cowley, P. & Stuart, M. (2004) 'Parliament: More Bleak House than Great Expectations', *Parliamentary Affairs*, 57:2, 301-314.

Cowley, P. & Stuart, M. (2005) 'Parliament: Hunting for Votes,' *Parliamentary Affairs*, 58:2, pp. 258-291.

Denton, M. & Flinders, M. (2005) *Democracy, Devolution and Delegated Governance in Scotland: Regional and Federal Studies*, (forthcoming).

Electoral Commission & Hansard Society (2004) *An Audit of Political Engagement* (London).

Electoral Commission & Hansard Society (2005) *An Audit of Political Engagement 2* (London).

Evans, P. (2004) 'The Human Rights Act and Westminster's Legislative Process', in Brazier, A. (ed.) *Parliament, Politics and Law Making* (London: Hansard Society).

Flinders, M. (2000) 'The Enduring Centrality of Individual Ministerial Responsibility Within the British Constitution', *Journal of Legislative Studies*, 6:3, 73-91.

Flinders, M. (2001) *The Politics of Accountability in the Modern State* (London: Ashgate).

Flinders, M. (2002) 'Shifting the Balance? Parliament, the Executive and the British Constitution', *Political Studies*, 50:2, pp. 23-42.

Flinders, M. (2003) 'New Labour and the Constitution' in Ludlam, S. & Smith, M. (eds.) *New Labour: Politics and Policy Under Blair* (London: Palgrave).

Flinders, M. (2004a) 'Icebergs and MPs: Delegated Governance and Parliament', *Parliamentary Affairs*, 57:4, 767-784.

Flinders, M. (2004b) 'Distributed Public Governance in the European Union', *Journal of European Public Policy*, 11:3, 520-544.

Flinders, M. (2004c) 'Distributed Public Governance in Britain', *Public Administration*, 82:4, pp. 883-909.

Flinders, M. (2005a) 'The Politics of Public-Private Partnerships' *British Journal of Politics and International Relations*, 7:2, pp. 543-567.

Flinders, M. (2005b) 'Majoritarian Democracy in Britain: New Labour and the British Constitution' *West European Politics*, 28:1, pp. 62-94.

Gay, O. (2005a) 'Making the Commons fit for the Twenty-First Century' in Baldwin, N. (ed.) *Parliament in the Twenty First Century* (forthcoming, London: Methuen).

Gay, O. (2005b) 'MPs Go Back to Their Constituencies', *Political Quarterly*, 76:1, 57-66.

Gregory, D. (1999) 'Style Over Substance? Labour and the Reform of Parliament', *Renewal*, 7:3, 42-50.

Hansard Society (1992) *Making the Law*, (London) [The Rippon Commission].

Hansard Society (2001) *Parliament: Making Government Accountable* (London: Vacher Dod) [The Newton Commission].

Hazell, R. (2001) 'Reforming the Constitution', *Political Quarterly*, 72:1, 39-50.

Hennessy, P. (1996) 'Teething the Watchdogs: Parliament, Government and Accountability', in *Muddling Through: Power, Politics and the Quality of Government in Post-War Britain* (London: Indigo).

Hennessy, P. (2004) 'An End to the Poverty of Aspirations? Parliament since 1979', First History of Parliament Lecture, Attlee Suite, Portcullis House, London 25 November 2004.

Hood, C. (2002) 'The Risk Game and the Blame Game', *Government and Opposition*, 37: 1, 15-37.

Hurd, D. (1997) 'The present usefulness of the House of Commons', *Journal of Legislative Studies*, 3:3, 1-9.

Institute of Public Policy Research (2004) *Opening It Up: Accountability and Partnerships* (London: IPPR).

Judge, D. (1993) *The Parliamentary State* (London: Sage).

Kennon, A. (2000) *The Commons: Reform or Modernisation?* (London: Constitution Unit).

King, A. (1996) *Is Britain a Well Governed Country?* (London: Lloyds TSB Forum).

Lord Alexander of Weedon (2000) *Can the Lords be the New Guardians of our Democracy* (London: The Constitution Unit).

Major, J. (2003) *The Erosion of Parliamentary Government* (London: Centre for Policy Studies).

Marquand, D. (2000) 'Revisiting the Blair Paradox', *New Left Review*, 3 May/June, 73-79.

McHugh, D. (2004) 'Parliament, Government and the Politics of Legislative Reform', in Brazier, A. (ed.) *Parliament, Politics and Law Making* (London: Hansard Society).

Morrison, J. (2001), *Reforming Britain* (London: Reuters).

Norton, P. (1983) 'The Norton View', in Judge, D. (ed.) *The Politics of Parliamentary Reform.* (London: Heinemann).

Norton, P. (2000a) *Strengthening Parliament The Report of the Commission to Strengthen Parliament* (London: The Conservative Party).

Norton, P. (2000b) 'Reforming Parliament in the United Kingdom', *Journal of Legislative Studies*, 6:3, 1-15.

Norton, P. (2004) 'Parliament and Legislative Scrutiny: An Overview of Issues in the Legislative Process', in Brazier, A. (ed.) *Parliament, Politics and Law Making* (London: Hansard Society).

Norton, P. (2005) 'Cohesion without Discipline: Party Voting in the House of Lords', *Journal of Legislative Studies*, forthcoming.

Parliament First (2003) *Parliament's Last Chance* (London).

Pollock, A., Shaoul, J., Rowland, D., & Player, S. (2001) *Public Services and the Private Sector* (London: Catalyst).

Riddell, P. (2000) *Parliament under Blair* (London: Politicos).

Riddell, P. (2004) 'Playing Ball and Raising the Game', *House Magazine*, 10 May 2004.

Rogers, R., & Walters, R., (2004) *How Parliament Works* (London: Pearson).

Rush M., & Ettinghausen C. (2002) *Opening Up The Usual Channels* (London: Hansard Society).

Seaton, J., & Winetrobe, B. K. (1999) 'Modernising the Commons', *Political Quarterly*, 70:2.

Shaw, E. (2004) 'What matters is what works: the Third Way and the Private Finance Initiative' in Hale, S., Leggett, W., & Martell, L. (eds.) *The Third Way and Beyond* (Manchester: Manchester University Press).

Smith-Hughes, A. (2001) *Parliament, the City and Financial Regulation* (London: Hansard Society).

Tant, A. (1990) 'The Campaign for Freedom of Information: a participatory challenge to elitist British government', *Public Administration*, 68, 477-491.

Taylor, A. (1996) 'New Politics, New Parliament', speech to Charter 88, 14 May 1996.

Tyler, P. (2003) *Britain's Democratic Deficit: Constitutional Reform – Unfinished Business* (London: Centre for Reform).

Tyrie, A. (2000) *Mr Blair's Poodle: An agenda for reviving the House of Commons* (London: Centre for Policy Studies).

Tyrie, A. (2004) *Mr Blair's Poodle goes to War* (London: Centre for Policy Studies).

Waldegrave, W. (1995) 'The Future of Parliamentary Government', *Journal of Legislative Studies*, 1:2, 173-177.

Weir, S. & Wright, A. (1996) *Power to the Back Benches?* (London: Scarman Trust/Democratic Audit).

Wright, A. (2000) *The British Political Process* (London: Routledge).

Wright, A. (2004) 'Prospects for Parliamentary Reform', *Parliamentary Affairs*, 57:4, 867-876.

Government and Parliamentary Publications

Cabinet Office, *Improving the Way the UK Handles European Legislation*, 2002.

Committee on International Development (2001-2002) *Evidence from the Prime Minister*, HC 984.

Foreign Affairs Committee (1998-1999) *Sierra Leone*, HC 116.

Foreign Affairs Committee (2000-2001) *Work of the Committee during the Present Parliament: A Progress Report*, HC 78.

Foreign Affairs Committee (2002-2003) *The Decision to go to war in Iraq*, HC 813.

Foreign Affairs Committee (2003-2004) *Implications for the Work of the House and its Committees of the Government's Lack of Co-operation with the Foreign Affairs Committee's Inquiry into The Decision to go to War in Iraq*, HC 440.

Government Response to the First Report from the Liaison Committee on Shifting the Balance: Select Committees and the Executive (2000) (London: HMSO), Cm. 4737.

Government Response to the Procedure Committee Report on Parliamentary Questions (HC622) (2002) (London: HMSO), Cm. 5628.

HM Treasury (2000) *Public Private Partnerships – the Government's Approach* (London: HMT).

HM Treasury (2003) *PFI: Meeting the Investment Challenge*.

House of Lords' Committee on the Constitution (2003-2004) *The Regulatory State: Ensuring Its Accountability*, HL 68.

House of Lords' Committee on the Constitution (2003-2004) *Parliament and the Legislative Process*, HL 173-I.

Joint Committee on Human Rights (2003-04), *The Meaning of Public Authority Under the Human Rights Act*, HL 39, HC 382.

Joint Committee on Financial Services and Markets, (1998-99) *Draft Financial Services and Markets Bill*, HC 328.

Joint Committee on Parliamentary Privilege (1998-99), *Parliamentary Privilege*, HC43-I, HL 214-I.

Liaison Committee (1999-2000) *Shifting the Balance: Select Committees and the Executive*, HC 300.

Liaison Committee (1999-2000) *Independence or Control? The Government's Reply to the Committee's First Report of Session 1999-2000 – Shifting the Balance: Select Committees and the Executive* HC 748.

Liaison Committee, (2000-2001) *Shifting the Balance – Unfinished Business*, HC 321.

Liaison Committee (2001-2002) *The Work of the Select Committees 2001*, HC 590.

Liaison Committee (2001-2002) *Select Committees: Modernisation Proposals*, HC 692.

Liaison Committee (2001-2002) *Oral Evidence given by the Rt. Hon. Tony Blair MP*, HC 1095.

Liaison Committee (2002-2003) *Oral Evidence given by the Rt. Hon. Tony Blair MP*, HC 334.

Liaison Committee (2002-2003) *The Work of the Select Committees 2002*, HC 558.

Liaison Committee (2003-2004) *Oral Evidence given by the Rt. Hon. Tony Blair MP*, HC 310.

Liaison Committee (2003-2004) *The Work of the Select Committees 2003*, HC 446.

Liaison Committee (2003-2004) *Oral Evidence given by the Rt. Hon. Peter Hain MP taken before the Liaison Committee, 19 October 2004*, HC 1180.

Liaison Committee, (2004-05), *Annual Report for 2004*, HC 419.

Local Government and the Regions Committee (2001-2002) *The Attendance of Lord Birt at the Transport, Local Government and the Regions Committee*, HC 655.

Memorandum submitted by the Leader of the House (2001-2002) *Modernisation of the House of Commons: A Reform Programme for Consultation*, HC 440.

Modernisation Committee (1997-98) *The Legislative Process*, HC 190.

Modernisation Committee (1997-98) *Explanatory Material for Bills*, HC 389.

Modernisation Committee (1997-98) *Carry-Over of Public Bills*, HC 543.

Modernisation Committee (1997-98) *Scrutiny of European Business*, HC 791.

Modernisation Committee (2001-2002) *Select Committees*, HC 224.

Modernisation Committee (2001-2002) *Modernisation of the House of Commons: A Reform Programme*, HC 1168.

Modernisation Committee (2003-2004), *Programming of Bills*, HC 1222.

Modernisation Committee (2003-2004) *Connecting Parliament with the Public*, HC 368.

Modernisation Committee (2004-2005) *Scrutiny of European Business*, HC 465-I.

Public Administration Select Committee (1997-1998) *Ministerial Accountability and Parliamentary Questions* HC 820.

Public Administration Select Committee (1998-1999) *Quangos*, HC 209.

Public Administration Select Committee (1998-1999) *Ministerial Accountability and Parliamentary Questions*, HC 821.

Public Administration Select Committee (2000-2001) *Ministerial Accountability and Parliamentary Questions*, HC 61.

Public Administration Select Committee (2000-2001) *Improving the Rule Book*, HC 235.

Public Administration Select Committee (2000-2001) *Special Advisers – Boon or Bane?*, HC 293.

Public Administration Select Committee (2000-2001) *Mapping the Quango State*, HC 367.

Public Administration Committee (2001-2002) *Ministerial Accountability and Parliamentary Questions: The Government's Response to the Committee's Second Report of Session 2000-2001*, HC 464.

Public Administration Select Committee (2001-2002) *Ministerial Accountability and Parliamentary Questions*, HC 1086.

Public Administration Select Committee (2002-2003) *Ministerial Accountability and Parliamentary Questions: The Government's Response*, HC 136.

Public Administration Select Committee (2003-2004) *Ministerial Accountability and Parliamentary Questions*, HC 355.

Public Administration Select Committee (2003-2004) *Oral Evidence given by Rt. Hon. Lord Butler of Brockwell on 21 October 2004*, HC 606-vi.

Public Administration Select Committee (2003-2004) *Ministerial Accountability and Parliamentary Questions: Government Response*, HC 1262.

Public Administration Select Committee (2004-2005) *Ministerial Accountability and Parliamentary Questions*, HC 449.

Public Service Committee (1995-1996) *Ministerial Accountability and Responsibility*, HC 313.

Public Service Committee (1996-1997) *Government Response to the Second Report from the Committee (Session 1995-1996) on Ministerial Accountability and Responsibility*, HC 67.

Public Service Committee (1996-1997) *Ministerial Accountability and Responsibility*, HC 313.

Procedure Committee (1984-85), *Public Bill Procedure*, HC 49.

Procedure Committee (1995-1996) *Delegated Legislation*, HC 152.

Procedure Committee (1999-2000) *Delegated Legislation*, HC 48.

Procedure Committee (2001-2002) *Parliamentary Questions*, HC 622.

Procedure Committee (2002-2003) *Delegated Legislation: Proposals for a Sifting Committee*, HC 50.

Second Report of the Procedure Committee (2002-2003) *Delegated Legislation: Proposals for a Sifting Committee, the Government's Response to the Committee's First Report*, HC 684.

Procedure Committee (2003-2004) *Joint Activities with the National Assembly for Wales*, HC 582.

Procedure Committee, Fourth Report (2003-04) *Programming of Legislation*, HC 325.

Procedure Committee (2003-2004) *Joint Activities with the National Assembly for Wales: The Government's Response to the Committee's Third Report*, HC 681.

Response of the Secretary of State for Foreign and Commonwealth Affairs to the Ninth Report of the Foreign Affairs Committee, Session 2002-2003 – The Decision to go to war in Iraq (2003) (London: HMSO), Cm. 6062.

Report of the Inquiry into the Circumstances Surrounding the Death of Dr David Kelly C.M.G., Ordered by the House of Commons to be printed 28 January 2004, (London: HMSO), HC 247.

Report of the Inquiry into the Export of Defence Equipment and Dual-Use Goods to Iraq and Related Prosecutions (2000-2001) HC 115.

Report from the Select Committee on Sittings of the House (1991-92) HC 20, [The Jopling Report].

Select Committee on the Constitution (2003-2004) *The Regulatory State: Ensuring its Accountability: The Government's Response*, HL 150.

Science and Technology Committee (2002-2003) *The Scientific Response to Terrorism*, HC 415.

Science and Technology Committee (2003-2004) *Annual Report 2003*, HC 169.

Transport, Local Government and the Regions Committee (2001-2002) *The Attendance of a Minister from HM Treasury before the Transport, Local Government and The Regions Committee*, HC 771.

Treasury Committee, (1998-99), *Financial Service Regulation*, HC 73.

Further publications from the HANSARD SOCIETY

Members Only? Parliament in the Public Eye, the Report of the Hansard Society Commission on the Communication of Parliamentary Democracy
(ISBN 1 900432 77 2), £25 (discount for students and others), May 2005
Chaired by Lord Puttnam, the Commission examines whether Parliament is failing in its democratic duty to communicate with the electorate. The report looks at the need to re-establish the crucial link between Parliament and the people, and sets out a practical route for much needed change.
The report is available from Dod's Parliamentary Communications.
To order, e-mail hansard@dods.co.uk

Parliament, Politics and Law Making: Issues and Developments in the Legislative Process (edited by Alex Brazier)
(ISBN 0 900432 57 8), £20, December 2004
To follow up its influential 1992 report, *Making the Law*, the Hansard Society has published a collection of essays exploring recent issues and developments in the legislative process.

Making the Law: The Report of the Hansard Society Commission on the Legislative Process
(ISBN 0 900432 24 1), £16, 1992
An authoritative text on the UK legislative process whose recommendations have been extremely influential within Parliament and Government.

Political Blogs – Craze or Convention? (Ross Ferguson and Milica Howell)
(ISBN 0 900432 47 0), £5, July 2004
Report examining the phenomena of political blogging.

A Tale of Two Houses – The House of Commons, the Big Brother House and the people at home (Stephen Coleman)
(ISBN 0 900432 07 1), £10, June 2003
A study examining the attitudes of 'political junkies' and Big Brother fans to politics, politicians and each other.

Parliament at the Apex: Parliamentary scrutiny and regulatory bodies (Alex Brazier)
(ISBN 0 900432 96 9), £7.50, February 2003
Report looks at Parliament's relationship with regulatory bodies.

Opening Up the Usual Channels (Michael Rush and Clare Ettinghausen)
(ISBN 0 900432 86 1), £10, December 2002
Based on original research into the people, personalities and systems that organise business in Parliament.

**Publications can be ordered from hansard@hansard.lse.ac.uk
or 020 7395 4008 (fax) or by post from
the Hansard Society, LSE, 9 Kingsway, London WC2B 6XF**